Teachers Act Up!

Teachers Act Up!

CREATING MULTICULTURAL LEARNING
COMMUNITIES THROUGH THEATRE

Melisa Cahnmann-Taylor and Mariana Souto-Manning

Foreword by Johnny Saldaña

Afterword by Kris D. Gutiérrez

TEACHERS
COLLEGE
PRESS

Teachers College, Columbia Univerity
New York and London

Published by Teachers College Press, 1234 Amsterdam Avenue, New York, NY 10027

All photos by Monira Al-Haroun Silk.

Portions of Chapter 5 from "The Power and Possibilities of Performative Critical Early Childhood Education," by M. Souto-Manning, M. Cahnmann-Taylor, J. Dice and J. Wooten, January 10, 2008, *Journal of Early Childhood Teacher Education, 29*(4), pp. 309–325. Copyright 2008 by Taylor & Francis. Reprinted by permission of the publisher (Taylor & Francis Ltd., http://www.tandf.co.uk/journals).

Library of Congress Cataloging-in-Publication Data

Cahnmann-Taylor, Melisa.
  Teachers act up! : creating multicultural learning communities through theatre / Melisa Cahnmann-Taylor and Mariana Souto-Manning ; foreword by Johnny Saldaña ; afterword by Kris D. Gutiérrez.
    p. cm.
  Includes bibliographical references and index.
  ISBN 978-0-8077-5073-5 (pbk : alk. paper) — ISBN 978-0-8077-5074-2 (cloth : alk. paper)
    1. Multicultural education—United States.   2. Theater—Study and teaching—United States.   3. Drama in education—United States.   4. Critical pedagogy—United States. I. Souto-Manning, Mariana.   II. Title

  LC1099.3.C34 2010
  370.117—dc22

                                                                      2010000350

ISBN 978-0-8077-5073-5 (paper)
ISBN 978-0-8077-5074-2 (hardcover)

Printed on acid-free paper
Manufactured in the United States of America

16   15   14   13   12   11   10   8   7   6   5   4   3   2   1

We dedicate this book to the life and legacy of
Augusto Boal
(April 6, 1931—May 2, 2009)

Maybe the theatre in itself is not revolutionary,
but these theatrical forms are without a doubt
a *rehearsal of revolution.*
—Augusto Boal, *Theatre of the Oppressed*

Contents

Foreword

FOR AN IN-SERVICE teachers' workshop in arts education several years ago, one of my colleagues hurriedly prepared an overhead transparency one morning for his presentation that day. He didn't proofread the text before he printed the plastic sheet, however, and within the bullet-pointed notes there was a misspelling of the word *education* that read:

eduaction

The crowd of teachers snickered at the mistake when we saw it projected on the screen. The workshop presenter laughingly apologized for the error and proceeded with his lecture.

But as his presentation continued, I couldn't take my eyes off the misspelled word, and I slowly realized that "eduaction" was why we were all there. The word reconfigured itself in my mind to appear as:

eduACTION

All of a sudden, there was a crystallizing moment of synthesis, when my personal-practical knowledge and readings of Paulo Freire, Augusto Boal, and other practitioners of multicultural education, arts education, and theatre for social change came together. Yes, I thought: eduACTION, not "education," is what we should be teaching in our classrooms. ACTION is doing; ACTION is on-your-feet; ACTION is standing up for your rights; ACTION is making change happen. And eduACTION is teaching and learning how to take action that makes the world a better place for the communities in which we coexist.

A Google search of the unique term informed me that other organizations and individuals have already discovered eduACTION as a new perspective on traditional pedagogy. Some sites use it purposefully to declare their progressive vision, but other sites have simply misspelled the original word. What this suggests is that we should not be making careless mistakes with "education," for there is too much at risk and too much human life at stake.

Teachers Act Up! is eduACTION at its best. Melisa Cahnmann-Taylor and Mariana Souto-Manning have documented their in-service teacher workshops in Theatre of the Oppressed with elegance and solid grounding in the relevant literature. They share their participants' career-changing experiences and responses in the teachers' own words—words that are heartfelt, in pain, and with hope. The coauthors are multicultural eduACTION's finest ambassadors for showing how improvisational theatre is a democratic medium for bodies and voices—the actor's and eduACTOR's tools of the trade—to express what is deep within and around us.

To be an eduACTOR in the field of eduACTION means possessing heightened consciousness of one's self and what it takes to make a difference for diverse groups of young people in the classroom. To be an eduACTOR means taking risks on a daily basis to intercede when injustices occur. To be an eduACTOR means envisioning multiple possibilities for solving a single problem. And to be an eduACTOR means performing in the world as if we are pivotal members of its ensemble, but those who also support our fellow players on stage.

If "teaching is performance," as the saying goes, then *all* teachers have the ability—indeed, the right and joy—to eduACT.

—Johnny Saldaña, Arizona State University

Acknowledgments

During the time we have spent Acting Up! and writing this book, we had wonderful individuals around us who influenced and inspired us. We would like to thank all who joined us in this journey. Below, at the risk of omitting important ones, we acknowledge some for their paramount influence, as they have ultimately become part of this project.

First we would like to acknowledge the support and love of our husbands, Jason Taylor and Dwight Manning, who during these years have given us support and encouragement to do the work in which we believe. Without them, this book would not exist.

We are grateful to the Transition to Teaching federal grant program for helping to fund the Teachers for English Language Learners (TELL) project upon which this work is based and to Dr. Betsy Rymes, who was the person who envisioned and secured federal funding. Betsy encouraged us to use theatre for our formative evaluation of bilingual teachers' progress, collaborated on early publications related to performance-based teacher education (Cahnmann, Rymes, & Souto-Manning, 2005; Rymes, Cahnmann-Taylor, & Souto-Manning, 2008), and continues to be one of our most highly valued friends in the field.

All TELL Scholars and early childhood, ESOL, and foreign language teachers who were part of this project gave their valuable time and commitment, providing significant insight to the alternating stresses and joys experienced by student teachers and certified teachers. We thank all these workshop participants for courageously sharing their lives with us and for daring to seek solutions performatively. A special thanks to all who graciously volunteered to be part of the photos that appear in the text: Mary, Alona, Yamileth, Constanza, Victoria, Elliott, Evelinne, Diana, Gabriela, João Vitor, Shakita, Iliana, Antonia, Kelly, Denise, Patricia, Magda, Alessandra, David, João Marcos, and Javier. We especially thank Monira Al-Haroun Silk, our TELL Scholar and artist extraordinaire, who took all photographs in this book, which capture the workshop's energy and enthusiasm. TELL associates and staff from 2003 to 2009 were also vital to the success of this project. Although we will not name all, we would like to express our sincere gratitude to Esperanza A. Mejía-Quijano, who coordinated many aspects of the project, including the facilitation of several caring interviews that inform this book.

Many graduate students helped us along the way. We would like to acknowledge the participation of all, but specifically Jennifer Wooten and Jaime Dice, coauthors on two articles that inform Chapter 5 in this text (Cahnmann-Taylor, Wooten, Souto-Manning, & Dice, 2009; Souto-Manning, Cahnmann-Taylor, Dice, & Wooten, 2008). We are indebted to them for their insight and collaboration. In addition, we express our heartfelt gratitude for all Jennifer Wooten did in every aspect of the project—going above and beyond any expectations, collecting data, Joking with us, and playing multiple roles that made this book possible, including her extraordinary direction during the photo shoot.

Augusto Boal's books and workshops, particularly *Games for Actors and Non-Actors* (1992), have directly informed the writing of this book. We are indebted to Boal's writing and teaching as well as numerous other "Jokers" who have helped us learn along the way, including Betty Smith Franklin, Julian Boal, Mark Weinblatt, Doug Patterson, Emi Garzitto, Claudia Kaiser-Lenoir, and Johnny Saldaña. Johnny Saldaña, thank you for the poetic and inspirational Foreword. We, too, believe in edu*ACTION*!

We offer our sincere gratitude to Meg Lemke and Susan Liddicoat, our Teachers College Press editors, for their patience, thoroughness, and encouragement. You provided the support we needed to move forward. We are grateful to numerous colleagues for their support and enthusiasm, underlining our gratitude to Bob Fecho, the first person to read our initial proposal and offer words of encouragement and questions to ponder. We also thank Donna Alvermann and Celia Genishi for encouraging us to seek a contract with Teachers College Press, and Sonia Nieto and Carol Lee for their supportive words. Finally, thank you to Kris Gutiérrez for her ongoing insight and care.

Our deepest gratitude goes to our children, Oren and Liya Cahnmann Taylor, and Lucas and Thomas Souto Manning. We hope you feel proud of our work and that you have teachers who will dare to Act Up! and perform change, making sure there are classrooms and schools that honor the voices of those who teach and learn within them.

Learning from Conflict, Performing Change

I can't wait until our next "therapeutic session" together. I realize how much our games and performances help every time I am face-to-face with the "surreal" in the classroom. It does something to my subconscious that helps me take and change things with sympathy and with a sense of humor.
—Act Up! Participant Cristina del Carmen

WHETHER WE ARE challenging test-driven curricula, administrative decisions that may be culturally biased, or our own assumptions about diverse learners and their families, our work as multicultural educators is never done. There is always a blind spot left to be revealed, always a curricular change to make learning more inclusive and democratic. To affect change in our school systems so they become more culturally responsive to diverse student populations and welcoming to diverse teachers, we must learn to communicate through conflict, breaking down barriers to social change.

But how can teachers face what Cristina referred to as "the surreal"—
everyday challenges and dilemmas in the classroom—with hope, compassion, and a sense of humor? For example, what do you do if you are an
elementary ESOL (English for Speakers of Other Languages) teacher working 10-hour days teaching and preparing lessons, while your cooperating
language arts teacher spends much of her school day shopping online and
assigning worksheets? What do you do when day after day a student in
your third-period world history class gets out of her chair to start dancing,
distracting her classmates and disrupting your instructional goals? What
do you do when your Spanish foreign language classroom becomes desig-
nated as a "study hall" and over half the students in your room have no
interest in studying language or generally being in school? Finally, when
you are an immigrant teacher yourself, how do you maintain your own
motivation when you're assigned to an administrator who claims not to
understand your instructional explanations due to your accented spoken
English?

Can teachers find hope for changing these situations, or are they perceived as fixed and unchanging? How can teachers navigate such struggles,
especially when there are issues of power involved? The cases above were
experienced by practicing teachers who told us that such scenarios presented real dilemmas in their professional lives, yet were seldom or never
addressed in their pre- or in-service learning.

No teacher education course can provide absolute answers to ongoing conflict in teachers' lives. We agree with Tollefson (1991) that struggle
cannot be ended but is "inherent to social systems in which groups have
different interests, and it is the source of social change" (p. 13). However,
when teachers experience struggle in isolation, they risk burnout, and we
all suffer from the loss of caring and competent teachers in the field. We
believe educators need forums for sharing some of their most urgent, day-
to-day dilemmas as they aim to create classroom and school climates that
affirm diversity and enhance students' sense of agency and voice in school
contexts and beyond (Nieto, 2007).

This book is about how professionals in education can engage in dialogue through differences of perspective, dialogue that feels meaningful
and sustaining, rather than exhausting and silencing. Our belief is that
teachers need more opportunities to rehearse the difficult conversations
they are likely to have again and again with their colleagues, students,
and friends; to hear their own scripts and find the potential to slow down
the face-to-face moments and re-envision their verbal and nonverbal
options for communication. Our own rehearsals with a wide variety of
teachers have led us to believe that this process can result in both personal and social transformation. We agree with Weinstein, Tomlinson-

Clarke, and Curran (2004) that it is the teacher educator's responsibility to "examine the kinds of cultural conflicts that are likely to arise in ethnically diverse classrooms, and to consider the best ways to help preservice [and in-service] teachers become multiculturally competent" (p. 27).

One approach to multicultural foundations courses has been the inclusion of a variety of texts that raise educators' consciousness of both visible and hidden forms of individual and institutional discrimination. These texts often include critical, theoretical readings and reports regarding successful practices in schools around the United States. These readings can and often do provide valuable information and insight into the diverse experiences of others and to the ways that structural forms of discrimination operate. Yet we have found that teachers need more than readings to affect real changes in their lives and in the lives of their students. In this book we introduce the ways we as teachers and teacher educators have used the dramatic and performing arts as tools in the process of developing critical multicultural learning communities.

We have taken inspiration from artists and revolutionaries that we can, in fact, work and act "as if" we lived in ideal contexts where every teacher's and every learner's full humanity are valued, where all school participants' voices are listened to and incorporated into authentic instructional experiences. But acting *as if* teachers have the power to make social change requires more than a new set of theories or case studies of unique learning environments. Teacher training for social change requires applied practice. In order to model for students the potential to be *who* they want to be and accomplish any variety of goals, teachers need to raise their awareness of the ways we physically and verbally communicate ourselves to others. This book is about using theatrical exercises when training teachers to Act Up! in their own personal and professional lives, allowing them to lead the next generation of educated change-agents to transformative ends.

ACTING UP

When teachers talk about students "acting up," they usually think about interruption or annoyance, like the student described above who dances during class time. However, moments of disruption can teach us so much, revealing situations that may require individual change (e.g., getting a student back in her chair) but perhaps larger structural changes as well (e.g., changing the design of the learning environment to be more active and participatory, more personally and culturally relevant). Perhaps we teachers need to learn from our students' small acts of classroom resistance, and rethink these "bad kid" behaviors as expressions of agentive voice (Macedo & Bartolomé, 1999). Acting up ourselves to fight back against structured forms of institutional discrimination may be necessary to promote change. For example, how might the Spanish foreign language teacher "act up" to her colleagues and administrators so that her classroom is treated as a place for serious learning rather than as a study hall? What options are available to a teacher who herself feels repeatedly discriminated against by an administrator with greater power? What constraints as well as power may an administrator feel from his supervisory positioning? In other words, what tools do educators require in order to practice and apply skills necessary to act up and perform in ways that bring about increased understanding and positive, productive change?

In school contexts where there are increasing numbers of students, parents, and staff from diverse racial, linguistic, national, and socioeconomic backgrounds, teachers are more likely to find themselves engaged in numerous conflicts yet without the critical, multicultural tools needed to communicate effectively. If there is anything universal about intercultural communication, it's the tendency for members of one cultural speech community to judge the words and actions of another by their own standards (Wolfson, 1998). Although we all act in different ways according to the situation—differently at family reunions from in the courthouse, for example—we are often unaware of the ways our own performance of self may either perpetuate or change a social situation. Recognizing the ways we can and do potentially "perform" ourselves in different contexts toward different ends can make us realize how we might strategically employ alternative performances to bring about more socially just outcomes. Both teachers and students can benefit from learning how to "act up" by increasing the diverse ways we can perform ourselves.

However, not only do different cultural standards lead to conflict, but there are also different degrees of power attached to those standards. Binary labels that assume static categories of race (White–Black), gender (male–female), language (English speaking–Non-English speaking), and so forth fail to address the extent to which communicative conflicts are also "forged in histories that are riven with differentially constituted relations of power" (Mohanty, 1989/90, p. 181). That is, when a Black female teacher, for example, feels threatened and silenced in the face of the aggressive behavior of a White male colleague, the moment-to-moment experience of oppression is also a part of systems of race, patriarchy, and gender reproduction inherited from generations past.

Many of the conflicts teachers experience with their students, students' parents, colleagues, administrators, and others are related to inequitable power relations (based on job status, race, class, language, and so forth) that are decades, even centuries, old. A structural-functionalist approach to these antagonisms views oppressive outcomes of conflict as a form of inevitable social control (Parsons, 1959). In contrast to structural-functionalist views, new turns in the critical, poststructural scholarship of possibility—particularly in critical discourse analysis, critical pedagogy, and critical multiculturalism—view conflict as dynamic, unpredictable, and filled with potential for change (Banks, 1995; Giroux, 1997; Kincheloe, 2005; Rymes, 2009). Despite the volume of texts written about interactional possibility, it is rare for teachers in professional development contexts to have an opportunity to rehearse lived experiences, explore alternative scripts, perform them, and prepare themselves for recurring opportunities to speak and act in a manner that is conscious, critical, and collective.

Although there are many opportunities to read about the possibility for individual and social transformation, there are too few opportunities for educators to rehearse possibility and prepare to make change happen. The question we have brought to our own work in educational contexts and the one we aim to answer in this book is, How do teachers and students actually transform their language and behavior to bring about social change? The premise of this book is that if teachers want to create positive change in the lives of their students, then teachers must first be able to create positive change in their own lives. When socialized to speak, talk, and act in certain professional, gendered, cultural, racial, and classed ways, is it possible to change? What do teachers of different cultural, racial, and linguistic identities see as their discursive options, especially when communicating with interlocutors of unequal power and status (e.g., a teacher speaking to a principal versus a teacher's assistant)? What processes are helpful in order for teachers to perform differently in times of conflict to bring about the most agentive forms of action in their lives and the lives of their students? In order for teachers not to be typecast as "nice," they need opportunities to rehearse alternative, edgier personas and to feel they've got a supporting cast behind them.

BREAKING THE FOURTH WALL—FROM SPECTATOR TO SPECT-ACTOR

In this book, we describe a professional development approach that merges the scholarship of critical pedagogy (Freire, 1970) with the theatrical, activist work of Augusto Boal (1979) called *Theatre of the Oppressed* (T.O.). We developed this approach when we were evaluating a grant program intended to increase the numbers of bilingual, mostly Spanish-English, teachers in Georgia. Our research team composed of teachers and teacher educators met regularly to talk about these educators' challenges and frustrations en route to becoming fully certified, bilingual teachers in the South, where there has been historically little foundation for bilingual education. Our discussions led to our considering meaningful practices to support *all* novice teachers, and especially those for whom English was not a first language and/or for teachers of color. Rather than just talking *about* struggles or performing them *for* teachers, we decided to get up from our chairs and re-enact them collaboratively. We employed Boal's term *spect-actors* to merge the binary terms of *spectator*, one who sits passively in an audience, with the term *actor*, one who performs in the dramatic scene. All participating educators were both spectators *and* actors, listening to one another's individual stories and how they connected to universal educational struggles for social change. Each teacher or spect-actor took turns portraying the protagonist teacher, rehearsing the possibilities for body language and discourse in moments of conflict with an antagonist other. In each narrative a bilingual teacher was the protagonist—the teacher who had to engage with colleagues who had ignored or mistreated English language learners; the teacher whose principal claimed not to understand the teacher's Spanish-accented English; the teacher whose paraprofessional made more rather than less work for her on a daily basis; and so on. Participating teachers engaged in consciousness-raising (e.g., Freire's [1970] *conscientização*) about their own subjectivities, learning to see that, despite the best of intentions, they could also become antagonists to others, how their words and actions could either perpetuate existing power imbalances or contest them.

These teachers acted up as themselves and each other in these theatrical rehearsals. They explored their real-life experiences of deep struggle with students, colleagues, parents, and others during and beyond the school day. Often these conflicts had haunted teachers outside of school work hours, keeping them awake at night, or, as in the case of one teacher participant, increasing her blood pressure and causing severe health problems. Teachers did not simply perform their lives on a proscenium stage; rather, they extended an invitation through the fourth wall between stage and audience, asking peers to replace them, providing alternative scripts and altering each drama's beginning, middle, and end. We began to see that if teachers could speak the words and perform the actions they wished they could in a safe rehearsal space, then this practice could actually make a difference for themselves and others in their real-life roles as educators.

Over the years, we have practiced these theatrical strategies with undergraduate and graduate students in early childhood education, foreign language, and TESOL (Teaching English to Speakers of Other Languages) classes; with College of Education faculty; and in numerous other contexts, from college courses to conference workshops, school site professional development seminars, and K–12 classrooms. Our work has shown how performance can be used to transform struggle into a deeply reflexive learning experience, one where *power-over* others is mediated and transformed to *power-with* others. This rearticulation of power makes it so one is not power*ful* or power*less*, but rather always involved in relations of power that are discursive and productive. That is to say that power is not something one has or doesn't have but something that is created by individuals in moment-to-moment conversation and interaction. We believe that if multicultural educators are going to facilitate a process whereby students can find their own voices and agency, then educators themselves must find *their* own voices, learning how to communicate across cultural, linguistic, socioeconomic, and other differences related to power.

READING THIS BOOK TOGETHER

Seeking to avoid just "talking the talk" of critical multiculturalism, we show in this book how performance strategies work in real practice. To accomplish this end, we employ a variety of arts-based tools for representation (Cahnmann-Taylor & Siegesmund, 2008; Saldaña, 2005), including narrative vignettes, transcripts of our focus groups turned into dramatic play scripts, detailed instructions for dramatic exercises, and photographic images. Such tools, we hope, will allow readers to come away with a thorough understanding of how we've used Theatre of the Oppressed strategies and how readers might adapt and use them in their own teaching and learning contexts and to what ends.

We have grouped the chapters in *Teachers Act Up!* into two parts. Part I consists of two chapters and seeks to provide the theoretical framework for our critical performative approach. Part II (Chapters 3–6) is the heart of the book. It contains information that will be useful to a wide variety of readers, including teacher educators, staff development leaders, and community activists who are looking for instructions and visuals that will help them understand and adapt Theatre of the Oppressed activities to their own contexts.

Finally, our Conclusion reflects on the implications of performance-based pedagogies in teacher education. Reviewing participants' surveys and interviews, we pinpoint the benefits and challenges of T.O. workshops. We explore the possibilities of Acting Up! for change in teacher education, as well as the risks in these times of testing pressures against liberatory practices.

   The Appendix includes a complete interview between a teacher educator and a teacher, regarding the teacher's experiences with Teachers Act Up! workshops. The interview reveals many of the powerful lessons that we (teacher educators and teachers) have learned from sharing Theatre of the Oppressed activities in our classrooms and workshops.

   Whether you are a teacher educator working with pre- or in-service teachers in multicultural foundations or content-area courses, an administrator looking for a new way to lead professional development, or a member of any learning community, this book's learning cases and embodied activities provide ways to put this work into practice in your own context. We encourage you to play with these ideas, redesign them for your own needs, and start acting up!

Theatre of the Oppressed as a Critical Performative Approach to Creating Multicultural Learning Communities: An Overview

THE TWO CHAPTERS in Part I provide background knowledge for the enactment of Theatre of the Oppressed techniques. In Chapter 1 we begin with the context in which we developed our performance-based practices. We situate this approach within a long line of work by teacher educators who prioritize teachers' personal, practical knowledge as foundational to critical, multicultural reflection on power, identity, and professional struggle in education.

Chapter 2 shifts the focus from critical multiculturalism, pedagogy, and performance more generally to Theatre of the Oppressed more specifically. Here we introduce readers to the lineage of Paulo Freire and his *Pedagogy of the Oppressed* (1970) as it connects to the foundations of our practice with Augusto Boal's (1979) Theatre of the Oppressed techniques. We provide an overview and an introduction to Boalian techniques. Finally, we review the literature related to how Theatre of the Oppressed strategies have been employed successfully in educational contexts and related fields.

Pushing the Chairs Aside:
How and Why We Got Started

ON WEEKDAY EVENINGS when most of the university campus shuts down for the day, the College of Education is aglow with bright fluorescently lit classrooms filled with pre- and in-service teachers enrolled in night courses pursuing certification, specialist, and/or graduate degrees. Like their peers around the country, many of these education students have worked long days in various instructional or other professional positions, left food on the table for their families, and come to us with totes full of course texts and papers. Others are full-time students, bright-eyed and eager to learn what they need to know in order to get their teaching careers off to a successful start. In one classroom, student teachers might be discussing a textbook on book clubs; in another class, topics include methods for teaching high school geometry or sharing third-grade social studies units on migrant workers and their relatively new presence in the Southeast.

One evening one of our students, "Marcia" (all names in this book are pseudonyms), arrived with bloodshot eyes and sagging shoulders. A new fourth-grade teacher taking a professional development course on campus, she had come from her school having just been lectured to for "30 minutes straight!" by a senior colleague because Marcia had sent a child to the office as punishment for stealing from her desk. "Mrs. Mean," Marcia's nickname for the school's discipline coach and fourth-grade team leader, believed that Marcia needed a stern lesson about the differences between situations that can and should be skillfully managed through a teacher's own discipline procedures and those that require an administrator's intervention. Holding back her tears, Marcia listened to what she should and should not do and learned that, despite her newly minted certificate in elementary education, colleagues like Mrs. Mean still did not (and might not ever) believe she was fully qualified to teach.

Marcia was experiencing what Bartolomé (2002) referred to as the "asymmetrical power relations among cultural groups" (p. 179). As a new teacher, Marcia felt as though Mrs. Mean and other colleagues marginalized her opinions, overlooked her strengths, and magnified her weaknesses. Her experience reflected "the arbitrariness of subordination and marginalization" (p. 183) that can happen to both adults and children depending on how they are socially positioned rather than according to actual qualifications and abilities. Social variables, such as race, class, gender, and age, among others, may have compounded the tensions between Marcia and her more senior colleague. At the same time, each of these social variables might have also been involved to create new points of connection and build trust.

Struggles, like the one Marcia experienced, happen on a daily basis between teachers and their colleagues, administrators, and parents, as well as between teachers and students. Yet there are seldom opportunities to address these complexities in teacher preparation. Unequivocally, these struggles experienced in isolation by teachers like Marcia drive many out of the profession, just as they can disproportionately drive some students out of school. Alternatively, these struggles can reinforce individuals' ethnocentrism rather than identifying the complex motivations that lead some to exert power over others in ways that feel unethical and unfair. We began to wonder about how our own professional development programs, both formal and informal, could integrate opportunities to elicit teachers' specific everyday lived realities. How could we begin to learn what was going on in their lives as student teachers or credentialed professionals? How could we help our students make connections to one another's stories related to identity and power without getting lost in generalities?

As explained in the Introduction, we sought to reframe our preparation programs so that participating teachers had more opportunities to examine the way power and ideology operated in their own lives and in the lives of their students, thereby impacting the potential for teaching and learning. We were influenced by the work of critical multicultural teacher educators and their emphasis on making ideology explicit (e.g., Banks, 1995; Bartolomé, 2002; Cochran-Smith & Fries, 2001; Darling-Hammond, 2007a; Grant & Sleeter, 1996). We also considered discussions among theatre activists and their commitments to social change (e.g., Rohd, 1998; Schutzman & Cohen-Cruz, 1990), and came to believe that teachers were often passive recipients of ideological scripts regarding what they could and could not do in their roles as educators. Based on our experiences with critical pedagogy and activist theatre, we developed our performance-based approaches to teacher learning.

STRESSES AND TENSIONS OF TEACHING IN MULTICULTURAL SCHOOLS WITHIN MONOCULTURAL NORMS

Through our program, Marcia was one of more than 50 teachers who have performed themselves and their antagonistic others over the last 6 years to collectively identify shared patterns among their individual struggles and negotiate possibilities for democratic change. Beyond simple interpersonal challenges, teachers shared the ways in which micro-level struggles between individuals (e.g., between colleagues such as Marcia and Mrs. Mean) were connected to larger tensions within the macro[-level], sociopolitical context. Often these tensions were related to ideological differences between multicultural and monocultural ways of being and relating to others in the world.

For example, the teachers with whom we worked struggled to meet the academic and emotional demands of their diverse students within the constraints of larger class sizes, scripted curricula, and pressures related to the increased presence of testing in the name of accountability. Test scores were believed to measure good teaching according to the No Child Left Behind Act of 2001 and determined the way federal funds were being dispersed (to sponsor "scientifically based" programs). This belief led many school districts and states to set up competitive environments, in which teachers were compared to one another, as were schools. A good school was defined according to its test scores; a good teacher, according to his or her students' performances and test scores. Teachers were given the message that schools were "culture-free" havens (Grant & Sleeter, 1996), and they were encouraged to teach the so-called "objective" curriculum as opposed to focusing on students as unique persons and full human beings (Crawford, 2004).

Many of our participating teachers worked in "high-need" schools, learning environments that were underresourced (as compared to more privileged communities), having inferior school facilities and less access to material resources (Darling-Hammond, 2007b). They recounted school conditions that contributed to their stress—e.g., overcrowding of classrooms, lack of technology, lack of books and even chairs (Kozol, 2007). In addition, there were multiple demands on teachers to teach in a specific way, to engage in "best practices," meaning monocultural practices (Goodwin, Cheruvu, & Genishi, 2008), to intervene and "fix" deficits that students brought to the classroom. Many of these teachers were employed in schools in which colleagues and administrators believed and practiced assimilation as a way of closing the achievement gap and held that diverse students were culturally deprived and needed immediate intervention (Carter & Goodwin, 1994).

In addition to the demands and complexities that focus group participants experienced in their roles as teachers in multicultural schools were the demands placed on them to find balance in their roles as family members. As more time was being asked of teachers to "fix" students and prepare them for exams, teachers were less able to spend quality time at home with their partners, spouses, children, friends, and/or aging parents.

Many of the teachers with whom we worked wanted to relieve some of the stresses associated with being pulled in so many directions. Many reported knowing that the models employed were not honoring their own diverse identities and those of their students, yet they did not know exactly what to do in the face of so many pressures. With these demands and so many others, teachers were akin to "pressure cookers" (Nieto, 2007). Unless they had a way to release that pressure and stress, they would explode. Unfortunately, amid such pressures, about half of the teachers in urban schools left the profession altogether within their first 5 years (Nieto, 2007).

THE PERSONAL AND INTERACTIONAL NATURE OF TEACHING IN A DIVERSE WORLD

Much of teaching is about personal relationships. Although the profession has been conceived by many as the transmission of knowledge, a major part of a teacher's role has to do with learning with and from others (Freire, 1970). We believe that teaching is fundamentally dependent on the quality of a teacher's relationships with others (be it parents, students, colleagues, administrators, or assistants). The quality and depth of these relationships impact what happens in the classroom and contribute to teachers' stress and doubts regarding their ability to shape and control their own lives (Kincheloe, 2008).

Such common everyday relationships can become more complex as individuals from multiple backgrounds—e.g., in terms of race, ethnicity, language, religion, ability, sexuality, and so forth—find themselves negotiating what it means to teach and learn in diverse schools (Ball, 2006). While it was once believed that differences in the United States would blend together in the public school melting pot, in reality many students and families have experienced a process of erasure (Valenzuela, 1999). A relationship of school culture over home culture became a defining factor in this assimilationist process that sought to "cure" diverse students of their differences in order to prepare them to succeed academically in the monocultural environment of school.

To move away from this faulty melting pot ideology that sought to assimilate and Americanize students and families, multicultural education was established during the civil rights movement of the 1960s and 1970s. It was partly a result of the legacy of W.E.B. Du Bois and other ethnic scholars (Banks, 1995). Multicultural education focused on reframing cultural and linguistic differences as resources instead of deficits in the teaching-learning process.

Multicultural education was originally based on the premise of respecting the humanity of each and every person. As such, it sought to prioritize teachers' and students' "personal, practical knowledge" as foundational to promoting change in teaching and teacher education (Connelly & Clandinin, 1988). It proposed that we must validate personal experience and appreciate the fact that "each is unique in their walking of this earth, each an entire universe, each somehow sacred. This recognition . . . demands that we embrace the humanity of every student" (Ayers, 2004, p. 35).

If multicultural education were to become a reality that would shape teaching and learning in our nation's schools, relationships and experiences of teachers would consequently come to the center of teaching and teacher education. According to Banks (2007), multicultural education aims "to improve race relations and to help all students acquire the knowledge, attitudes and skills needed to participate in cross-cultural interactions and in personal, social, and civic action that will help make our nation more democratic and just" (p. xii). Nevertheless, traditional models of teacher education do not consider the importance of such personal, social, and civic actions, which rest on a multitude of situated experiences and relationships.

Throughout the country, traditional models for preparing teachers focus on methods and curriculum implementation (Hughes, 1999). This is evidenced by the ways academic degree programs are designed—grounded in content-area methods such as math, science, and language arts instruction (Anderson, 2005). Pre-service teachers learn about best practices, implementing curricula, and teaching strategies. Although traditional teacher education programs give teachers the tools to teach the curriculum, they often do not fully address the social, emotional, and ideological contexts in which education occurs (Souto-Manning, Cahnmann-Taylor, Dice, & Wooten, 2008).

Nevertheless, teachers must negotiate relationships with individuals—both adults and young people—on a daily basis. New teachers with whom we worked over the course of 6 years have let us know that they often found themselves unprepared to negotiate critical, professional relationships with teacher aides, administrators, and parents, among others. In essence, we found that many teacher education programs seemed to leave new teachers unprepared for the possibility of clashing educational paradigms, culturally shaped beliefs, and personal characteristics (Cochran-Smith & Lytle, 1990; Darling-Hammond, 2000).

Figure 1.1 represents the traditional model of teacher education—a solution-oriented approach (Porfilio & Yu, 2006; Tom, 1997). This traditional form of teacher education is prevalent throughout the country (Souto-Manning, Cahnmann-Taylor, Dice, & Wooten, 2008). It portrays a hierarchical approach in which the professor and/or the textbook are considered to be the ultimate sources of and authorities for knowledge (Cahnmann, Rymes, & Souto-Manning, 2005; Rymes, 2009). Teacher educators are perceived as the holders of knowledge that must be mastered by pre- and in-service teachers in order to become effective and competent professionals. Curricula and syllabi revolve around traditionally defined texts, which often become the voice of authority. This model is solution-oriented in that it seeks to provide solutions to issues being explored—often scripted and decontextualized solutions coming from a text. This solution is fashioned in a monologic manner. There is no exchange of ideas or blurring of teacher educator and teacher roles. The teacher educator provides the solution based on published texts. While there might be talk, the talk can be categorized as a side-by-side monologue rather than a dialogic exchange of ideas (Allen, 2007). The texts selected for the course offer the solution. Finally, there is a cathartic release, the "this is how it's done" moment, as if all teachers' instructional dilemmas have been resolved. This Aristotelian catharsis results in teacher education that is disempowering and tranquilizing, adapting the individual to society (Boal, 1995), rather than facilitating empowering and agentive education.

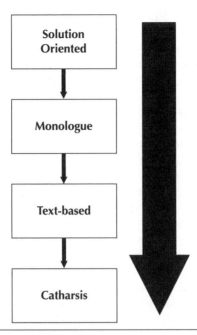

Figure 1.1. Traditional Model of Teacher Education
Source: Souto-Manning, Cahnmann-Taylor, Dice, & Wooten, 2008.

We are not assuming here that all teacher education programs follow the exact model illustrated by Figure 1.1, yet we have documented that it is a common model (Souto-Manning, Cahnmann-Taylor, Dice, & Wooten, 2008). By adhering to such models, new teachers come to rely on assigned texts and accept a subtle message that there is a specific protocol or procedure, a script for each situation (Cochran-Smith & Fries, 2001). This traditional way of educating teachers does not consider interactions or conflicts and, consequently, tends to result in frustration on the part of teachers who cannot seem to implement such canny and quick solutions in their classrooms and schools. Hence, this leads to the so-called disconnect or chasm between universities and schools, between teacher educators and teachers.

Furthermore, this traditional solution-oriented model goes directly against the premise of multicultural education. Seldom do pre-service and in-service teachers experience an educational environment that honors their own concrete, lived experiences with diversity, nor have they been asked to contemplate how teaching and learning are affected by differences in terms of identity and power or to engage in active social engagement

(Rhedding-Jones, 2002; Rust, 1999). The approach in which the teacher educator and course texts are presented as authorities reinforces the monocultural and assimilationist nature of teacher education classes (Cahnmann, Rymes, & Souto-Manning, 2005; Rymes, 2009).

FOCUSING ON CULTURALLY RESPONSIVE PRACTICES

Despite the commonness of monocultural teaching, as well as assimilationist and deficit perspectives, several studies have documented successful teaching of diverse children and pinpointed practices, beliefs, and stances that foster rethinking teacher education in culturally responsive ways. The following review of select studies helps us see how to engage in critical multiculturalism (Obidah, 2000), which links the dynamic concepts of culture, identity, and experience with an analysis of power structures and pedagogy. These studies portray a paradigm that frames differences in terms of resources and strengths that can be built upon (Goodwin, Cheruvu, & Genishi, 2008; Zentella, 2005).

Fennimore (2000), Hoffman (1996), and Sleeter and Bernal (2003) noted that little is truly known about how to do multiculturalism in schools. As we sought to engage in multicultural teacher education, we wanted to make sure not to fall into the trivialized infusion of celebrations and commemorations, while ignoring the everyday issues and tensions experienced by diverse teachers in their everyday lives. Instead of thinking of teachers in terms of what they were not able to do in their classrooms (in terms of deficits), we wanted to engage them in a rich multicultural experience that empowered them to understand themselves in relation to others. We must recognize that not only students but teachers as well are members of cultural groups, and their behaviors are consequently influenced by characteristics of these cultural groups. Once identified, such cultural differences contribute to more opportunities to expand multicultural competencies of all teachers and thus all students. The first step toward change is the awareness of one's cultural location. Although histories shape people, people also shape histories, live the present, and redirect futures. Power and identity are always socially negotiated constructs.

The studies below help us frame goals for a dialogic pedagogy. This kind of pedagogy blurs the role of teacher and learner (Freire, 1998a), positioning students as experts from whom much can (and should) be learned. They illustrate multiple paths to diverse solutions for culturally and linguistically complex classrooms. They illustrate how teachers move systematically toward multicultural ends.

Differences as Resources for Learning

In the mid-1990s, Gloria Ladson-Billings wrote the compelling and ground-breaking *The Dreamkeepers: Successful Teachers of African American Children*. In it, Ladson-Billings moved away from the model that blames students for their own failures as she documented the successful practices of eight teachers (African Americans and European Americans) who honored African American students in their classrooms. It is clear that even though these teachers came from different racial and cultural backgrounds and had different styles of teaching, they all shared the belief that students' poor performances in school were not due to the students' own inadequacies or deficits but because the quality of instruction they experienced was inappropriate and did not meet African American students' needs. Based on cases presented throughout the book, Ladson-Billings proposed that successful teachers identify African American students' interests, life experiences, and existing knowledge and make this the basis for a culturally relevant curriculum. For example, she showcased literacy instruction focused on children's love and knowledge of rap music, honoring students as translators between vernacular and standard varieties of English. Of utmost importance is Ladson-Billings's notion that successful teachers of African American students share "an overriding belief that students come to school with knowledge . . . [which] must be explored and utilized in order for students to become achievers" (1994, p. 52). Influenced by Ladson-Billings's (1994) work, Lee (2007), Ball and Lardner (2006), Howard (2006), and others have focused similar empirical attention on African American students' strengths as foundations for meaningful academic literacy instruction.

Angela Valenzuela (1999) documented the many ways in which schooling can be a subtractive process for students of Mexican descent. She drew upon culturally situated knowledge and enacted culturally relevant ways of teaching in classrooms. In her book *Subtractive Schooling: U.S.–Mexican Youth and the Politics of Caring*, Valenzuela employed a sociocultural-historical analysis of schooling, focusing on Mexican American students in a Houston, Texas, inner-city high school. She exposed the importance of social processes, which were mediated through students' lived experiences, to their academic achievement. She pinpointed the importance of creating and sustaining a culture of caring—in which teachers valued students' situated experiences and cultural knowledges—to Mexican-descent students' success. Valenzuela suggested that creating a culture of caring is key to fostering the academic success of Mexican American students. Successful teachers of Mexican-descent students, according to Valenzuela, enter into academic and emotionally productive spaces when they develop sustained relationships with students, honoring and embodying students' notions of caring.

Moll and Gonzalez (2004) have documented ways in which teachers became applied anthropologists, identifying the cultural patterns related to Mexican American students' home learning experiences (e.g., candy-making and flea-market vending) and building upon these experiences for their mathematics and literacy instruction.

Structured in a similar way to Ladson-Billings's work, Gilda Ochoa's (2007) study focused on the narratives of eight Latino teachers. She proposed that successful teachers of Latino students use power-conflict theories to explore and understand sociocultural, historical, structural, and ideological factors shaping the unequal experiences of Latinos in U.S. schools. Specifically, Ochoa wrote about the power of family support in encouraging resilience and resistance, the importance of mentors and supportive school officials, and the significance of nurturing individual determination. The teachers' own stories served as critiques of deficit theories of Latino students' learning. Ochoa explored the practices of tracking and high-stakes testing and their negative effects on both Latino students and their Latino teachers.

From a wider lens, Genishi and Goodwin's edited volume (2008) revealed several studies that documented teachers rethinking and "doing diversities" across race, class, ethnicity, culture, gender, sexuality, and religion. Being culturally situated, the studies in this text challenge the concept of "best practices." For example, in the chapter written by Sarsona, Goo, Kawakami, and Au (2008), a program called Keiki Steps illustrated the inherent cultural differences and conflicts between "best practices" and Hawaiian cultural values. In rethinking teacher education, Susi Long and colleagues (2008) wrote about how White teachers can go beyond their own worlds as a first step to understanding privilege and the importance cultural norms play in classroom life.

These are just a few studies that have documented the struggles and importance of teaching against the grain, of naming and challenging the injustices experienced by diverse children and their teachers in classrooms and schools throughout the country. They serve as affirmation that culturally responsive education can be done. We are aware, however, that in many school contexts, critical multicultural ways of teaching can often be a stressful and solitary journey.

Teachers' Personal, Practical Knowledge

We situate this book within a long line of work by teacher educators who prioritize teachers' personal, practical knowledge as foundational to critical, multicultural reflection on power, identity, and professional struggle in education (c.f., Gomez & Abt-Perkins, 1995; Gomez, 2002; Shulman & Mesa-Bains, 1993). Storytelling is a site for problem solving; consequently, as teachers tell their stories they problem solve (Allen & Hermann-Wilmarth, 2004; Ochs, Smith, & Taylor, 1996), opening up the potential for developing an awareness of their own constructions of culture as they analyze their own stories.

Teacher educators Mary Louise Gomez and Dawn Abt-Perkins have been asking for many years what happens when teachers tell stories about themselves and their work (Abt-Perkins & Gomez, 1993; Gomez, 1992; Gomez & Abt-Perkins, 1995; Gomez & Tabachnick, 1992). They have found that in telling teaching stories—narratives in which a teacher and her classroom practices play a central role—individuals can conduct a self-critique in which they can see themselves and their complex interactions with others in a fresh light. In particular, these researchers try to understand how telling teaching stories to their peers (over time and in a supportive setting) can assist teachers in puzzling through their behavior toward different students; questioning accepted schooling practices; unpacking the social, economic, and institutional forces against which children and their families struggle; and devising new ways to teach that invite all children to learn.

Linda Darling-Hammond (2007a) wrote that selecting generative data sets is necessary to engage in multicultural teacher education. That is, stories that shape the curriculum in teacher education must be generated in the classroom, from real interactions. Accessing the resources that preservice and in-service teachers bring to the teacher education classroom (or professional development workshop) is fundamental to engage in critical multicultural teacher education. "The clear exposition of how teachers [and teacher educators] can assemble such cultural data sets and the practice that draws upon them is a tremendous contribution to teacher education" (p. xx). In this book, we share our experience as we created multicultural communities through theatre, nurturing our collective abilities to see beyond our individual perspectives, "to put oneself in the shoes of the learner and to understand the meaning of that experience in terms of learning . . . perhaps the most important role of teacher preparation" (Darling-Hammond, 2008, p. 343).

WHY THEATRE? EXPLORING POSSIBILITIES IN MULTICULTURAL TEACHER EDUCATION

Much of the literature in multicultural education and teacher education reminds us that the status quo must change in order to pursue a fully humanizing pedagogy for all learners. Many of the empirical studies cited above and others in multicultural teacher research illuminate the fact that change is possible. However, seldom in this body of literature do we learn *how* this change might take place (Howard, 2006). In the fields of multicultural teacher training and research, we believe too much attention has been given to intellectual considerations and too little to other modalities, including the physical and the imaginative. We agree with Harman and French (2004) that "the collaborative and contextualized use of bodies in specific local spaces can help students and teachers to connect viscerally to the issues raised and analyzed in critical multicultural teacher education programs" (p. 107). For this reason, we have chosen to explore how theatre might be used as an invitation for the body to join the mind in a transformative approach to teacher education.

Pineau (2002) proposed the term *the ideological body* to represent the relationship between teachers' physical bodies and the cultural associations of language, race, class, gender, sexual orientation, ablebodiedness, and so forth that are imprinted on the human form. In traditional multicultural foundations courses, teachers are often asked to perform an oral presentation for a summative assessment of their abilities. Pineau argued for a shift from the body as performative spectacle to the body as a medium for experiential learning. Through a performative approach, teacher training may become a context not only for thinking about change but also for taking imaginative and embodied action.

Distinct techniques of process are needed for individuals to transform the ways they relate to others in a diverse world. Louis (2005) argued that "because performance itself is grounded in action, reflexivity, and dialogue, a critical performative pedagogy denies students the comfort of a quiet, object position" (p. 344). The challenging work in critical multicultural teacher training is to find ways for teachers to become subjects of their own learning, learning that may unsettle previously held thoughts, values, and beliefs systems. Delpit (1988) wrote that teachers "must learn to be vulnerable enough to allow our world to turn upside down in order to allow the realities of others to edge themselves into our consciousness" (p. 297). Cixous (1993) extended this to what it means to be fully human: "to be human we need to experience the end of the world. We need to lose the world, to lose a world, and to discover that there is more than one world and that the world isn't what we think it is" (p. 10).

Although performance pedagogy can be a mode for opening up an array of possibilities and perspectives, it also bears additional responsibilities upon the teacher educator: an obligation to learn more about how, when, and why performance serves as a mode of analysis, engagement, or critique (Warren, 1999). The next chapter of this book reviews the history and applications of a specific kind of critical, performative pedagogy, Theatre of the Oppressed (Boal, 1979), and its relationship to the critical pedagogical practices espoused by Paulo Freire (1970). We explore how the collective practice of these performance techniques can become a rehearsal for real dialogue and social action in teachers' lives.

The Oppressed or the Oppressor? How Much Power Does the Teacher Have?

WHAT IS OPPRESSION? The word *oppression* may elicit strong feelings and images for many people living in the United States. When asked to define *oppression*, educators attending one of our Theatre of the Oppressed workshops shared the following conversation:

> REGGIE: The word makes me think of dictatorship, like Stalin. (*Various assenting voices.*)
> MARISOL: Yeah, like Castro!
> REGGIE: (*shaking his head*) I don't experience that type of oppression in the classroom—I don't even think we can talk about that kind of oppression in the U.S.!

Teachers like Reggie (born in the United States) and Marisol (born in Cuba) who participated in our earliest performance workshops share a common definition of *oppression* that implies a top-down configuration of absolute power possessed and exercised by a privileged and authoritative few against the have-nots, or those in the majority who do not have power.

In the United States, we have a history of supporting revolutions against monarchies and dictatorships. Numerous books and films have portrayed how Americans have painstakingly fought to expand each citizen's civil rights to participate equally in the pursuit of liberty and justice for all, both at home and abroad. Indeed, most of us living in the United States do not see ourselves as a nation living beneath the authoritarian rule of a dictator. Rather, many position themselves as active participants and creators of a democratic fabric. Despite the perception that common citizens are active participants in a democratic society, perhaps what Foucault (1978) argued is true—that despite our belief that we live in a democracy, "we still have not cut off the head of the king" (pp. 88–89).

Augusto Boal (1979), like Foucault, believed that despite the absence of external despots,* we tend to carry "cops in our heads"—those voices that self-censor, controlling and limiting the extent to which we take liberatory, transformative actions. Foucault (1978)—and the 44th U.S. president Barack Obama, too, for that matter—have reminded us not to put too much faith in a democracy based solely on political elections, but that true democracy requires the active civic participation of its citizens, citizens who recognize that "negative forms of power" (Foucault, 2001, p. 123) are always possible, yet can also always be contested.

While Reggie, Marisol, and many other teachers may not identify with the word *oppression* or with being overtly oppressed themselves, they do experience power over themselves in the form of pressures and mandates that shape their classrooms and teaching practices. In addition, to complicate matters, teachers are often themselves the targets of stereotypes that portray them as oppressors or classroom dictators. Teachers are often perceived as carrying out the bidding of the state, helping to control the masses by enforcing the one-way transmission of state-mandated curriculum.

Paulo Freire (1970) identified "Banking Education," whereby teachers "deposit" information into students' "accounts," and the ways in which this model can weaken democratic participation. He wrote:

> In the banking concept of education, knowledge is a gift bestowed by those who consider themselves knowledgeable upon those whom they consider

---

*Although we write this from a U.S. perspective, we are also mindful of international readers who may be living under despotic regimes or perceive the U.S. government as one that is overtly or covertly oppressive.

to know nothing. Projecting an absolute ignorance onto others, a characteristic of the ideology of oppression, negates education and knowledge as processes of inquiry. The teacher presents himself to his students as their necessary opposite; by considering their ignorance absolute, he justifies his own existence. The students, alienated like the slave in the Hegelian dialectic, accept their ignorance as justifying the teacher's existence—but, unlike the slave, they never discover that they educate the teacher. (p. 53)

Rejecting this monologic, top-down style of education, Freire offered "problem-posing education" as an alternative, as a way to challenge the status quo. Freire wrote about a teaching philosophy that prides itself on blurring the roles of teacher and learner (Freire, 1998b). In applying this pedagogy, the teacher would base inquiry on learners' prior knowledge, experiences, and critical questions about his or her own community (Souto-Manning, 2010).

To initiate problem-posing and engage in dialogue with students, teachers immerse themselves into students' communities to learn about the students' lives and immediate struggles. They collect data in an ethnographic manner, and codify the relevant, representative, and recurring themes into situations (via pictures, vignettes, and so forth). These are called "generative themes," which reflect subjects of immediate relevance to students' lives. These generative themes are in turn collectively problematized as participants continuously try to identify larger issues shaping oppressive situations. Through dialogue and the consideration of a number of perspectives, participants problem solve and chart a plan for action, for transforming personal and/or social realms (Souto-Manning, 2005; 2007; 2009b).

For example, in Cahnmann's (2001; 2006) ethnographic study of a successful Nicaraguan-born teacher and her Puerto Rican students in North Philadelphia, critical pedagogy was based on generative themes of direct relevance to the participants' lives, such as national and local debates surrounding bilingual education and the contested sovereignty of the island of Vieques, Puerto Rico, occupied by the U.S. military. In Souto-Manning's teacher action research study (2009b), elementary school students engaged in problematizing the very issues that were frustrating them (seemingly segregated pull-out programs), engaging in dialogue and problem solving together. As a collective, 6- and 7-year-olds were able to change the way special education, gifted education, and ESOL were delivered, having a direct impact on their school lives.

Although there are studies (including those cited above and many others) that exemplify this sort of problem-posing pedagogy, teachers who aspire to engage in problem-posing forms of education may themselves feel consciously or unconsciously constrained by oppressive societal forces beyond their control. Debates about scripted curricula, mandated standardized tests, and "English only" are present in national media or in teacher workrooms. These and other external political forces can negatively impact a teacher's perception of him- or herself as one who nurtures both students' and teachers' voices for change. Nevertheless, there are hopeful spaces for embracing problem-posing education in public schools (Souto-Manning, 2009a; 2009b).

While a teacher in the United States may prefer not to identify her- or himself as someone who is "an oppressor" or "the oppressed," she or he may nonetheless be part of systems of power that implicitly or explicitly control or limit possibilities for participatory democracy. However, teachers may experience oppression in a more overt manner in a nationwide, sanctioned dictatorship. This was the case for Freire in 1960s Brazil where teachers had highly restrictive access to curricular choice due to a nationally mandated curriculum in which the teaching of sociology and philosophy—as subjects and topics shaping knowledge—were outlawed and could lead to imprisonment. At the same time, the teaching of moral education, civic education, and social organization—all organized around military principles—were at the forefront of the curriculum. Nonetheless, teachers in the United States often struggle with questions regarding who exerts power and control over whom within public school systems. These struggles influence what can and should occur in the classroom and signify opportunities for learning, growth, and change (Cowhey, 2006).

FROM PEDAGOGY TO THEATRE OF THE OPPRESSED: THE INFLUENCE OF PAULO FREIRE ON THE WORK OF AUGUSTO BOAL

Considering the specific context of 1960s Brazil, marked by authoritarian regimes and inequality, signaled by socioeconomic dichotomies of extreme poverty and wealth, it is little wonder why both Paulo Freire and Augusto Boal employed the term *oppressed* to describe the plight of the people with whom they first worked in South America. Their work emerged in a very unequal and oppressive system and society. While there was a dictatorship at the national level, this very structure was reproduced on smaller, more local scales. Some of the working conditions experienced by those in poverty were akin to slavery. For example, peasants worked in sugar mills and on farms for food and shelter, paying their employers for housing and exorbitantly priced food in isolated locales. Rich farmers made goods available to peasants by maintaining accounts at general stores that they ran on their own properties. These credit accounts grew much faster than the workers' wages. Soon, farmers had total control of workers, who could not leave because they owed money to their bosses and landlords.

Within this context, Theatre of the Oppressed was established in the 1960s by Brazilian theatre director and Workers' Party (Partido dos Trabalhadores [PT]) political activist Augusto Boal. Boal was inspired by the ideas of Paulo Freire, who published his concepts in his landmark treatise on education, *Pedagogy of the Oppressed* (1970). Boal (2005) described their relationship in an interview:

> Paulo Freire was a very good friend of mine, and he started more or less in the 1960s. Once we were talking to try to remember when we have met for the first time. We do not remember well. We had the impression that we have met for all our lives. And his work inspired me, of course, and did develop parallel one to another. But of course he wrote the *Pedagogy of the Oppressed* first, and by title *Theatre of the Oppressed* is a homage to him. (¶ 13)

In the 1960s, Boal's theatre troupe was performing Agit Prop Theatre, plays aimed at arousing dialogue among peasants in disempowered areas. After a show in the northeastern region of Brazil (home to Freire), a peasant came up to the actors and said, "Okay, if you think like that, come with us and let's fight the government" (Taussig & Schechner, 1994, p. 23). The spectator in the audience had been so moved by the performance, he believed in the play's resolution and asked the actors to take their rifles and go with him to the streets. The actors declined, admitting that their guns were fake, but the peasant replied, "We have enough real rifles for everyone" (p. 23).

This exchange was both an embarrassment and a revelation to Boal and served as the inspiration for changing his approach to politics and theatre. Boal realized that his plays did not present solutions he himself was prepared to carry out, and also that theatre could arouse the public to immediate social action. Boal grew critical of theatre that resulted in catharsis of emotion but led to inaction (Schutzman & Cohen-Cruz, 1994). It was no longer acceptable to consider the generative themes, problematize the larger issues shaping them, and dialogically seek solutions. As voiced by the peasant offering "real rifles," it was time to do, to change, to engage in social action. Boal wanted to create an aesthetic process in which those experiencing oppressive conditions and situations themselves could be in charge of generating their own solutions, judging their realities and consequences and arriving at collective action. Thus Theatre of the Oppressed was born in the Americas.

Theatre of the Oppressed has many contextually situated and fluid components, the discussion of which can be found in Boal's many different texts (1974; 1979; 1992; 1995; 1998; 2002; 2005). In Figure 2.1 we present an overview of the breadth of Boal's work, listing the titles and purposes of his many techniques and where further discussion is located in our text.

Because of such strong influences, Augusto Boal referred to Paulo Freire as his "last father" when Freire passed away on May 2, 1997 (Boal, 2005). It is easy to notice how Freire's theory permeated Boal's practice in *Theatre of the Oppressed* (Boal, 1979), a performative version of the concepts presented in *Pedagogy of the Oppressed* (Freire, 1970). Both Freire and Boal foregrounded generative themes to initiate dialogue and problematize everyday realities that oppressed the lower classes. For example, Freire believed that the best way to teach literacy practices to illiterate *favela* dwellers was to begin with generative sets of images and words that related to everyday community struggles; for example, a bottle of alcohol and the word *alcoholism* to generate meaningful engagements with written words of community importance; a painting of a rural worker laboring to represent the struggles of farm workers. Likewise, Boal wanted to create theatrical experiences that addressed real aspects of community struggles, recursive situations that oppressed people day in and day out.

While experimenting with nontraditional theatre methods in São Paulo, southeastern Brazil, Boal developed a more engaged and interactive form of theatre he called Forum Theatre. Instead of an audience reacting to plays only after they ended, Boal conceptualized the spectator as an active, co-generator of the drama's content and outcome. Instead of waiting for the curtains to draw in order to articulate their thoughts and reactions verbally, Boal invited spectators to become "spect-actors," a hybrid of spectator and actor. Under Boal's direction, spect-actors had the power to initiate scenarios based on recurring conflicts in their lives and to interrupt performances to offer alternative actions to the "Protagonist" character. Initially, this occurred in a more verbal way, as audience members would suggest actions to be performed by the professional actor playing the character/role. Later on, the true potential of the spect-actor came to life as a woman, frustrated that the professional actor could not understand her verbal suggestions, stepped onto stage and assumed the role of the oppressed character, the "scorned wife," herself (Boal, 1995, pp. 4–7).

Spect-actors became a common part of Boal's experiments, as those suggesting alternative courses of action were invited to step up and replace the actor on stage, playing the role of the oppressed Protagonist a different way. The idea of spect-actors as a role challenges the "fourth wall" division between stage and audience (akin to Freire's proposition that the roles of teachers and learners be blurred). By embodying such a role, Boalian theatre engages all participants equally in generating the plot of

Boalian T.O. Component	Purpose
Games for Actors and Non-Actors (Boal, 1992)	To develop body awareness and solidarity through creative, physical activity within a group. Theatre games are meant to work on both literal and metaphoric levels (discussed further in Chapter 3).
Image Theatre (Boal, 1979)	To undo the body's habits and expand one's possibilities for physical expression. Through the use of bodies as sculptural "clay," participants create images that reflect their perception of a situation or perspective on the world (discussed further in Chapter 4).
Forum Theatre (Boal, 1979)	To elicit three-part narrative structures detailing dramatic tensions between protagonists and antagonists. Participants are simultaneously spectators and actors, or *spect-actors*, stopping scenes and offering their own embodied scripts to bring about change in the dramatic outcome to advantage the protagonist (discussed further in Chapter 5).
Cop in the Head (Boal, 1995)	To explore internal voices, fears, oppressions that prevent participants from living fully (discussed further in Chapter 6).
Rainbow of Desire (Boal, 1995)	To move from one protagonist and one antagonist to explore the multivocality of a single individual with the various motivations behind one's spoken words and actions. Rainbow explores how one can simultaneously occupy the positions of the oppressor and the oppressed, challenging spect-actors to perform the range of character hues that inform any interactional moment (discussed further in Chapter 6).
Invisible Theatre (1979)	To stimulate a dialogue involving the public without their knowing it has been staged (discussed further in Chapter 6).
Legislative Theatre (1998/2004)	To draw out public opinion and create policy based on collective support (discussed further in Chapter 6).

Figure 2.1. Theatre of the Oppressed and Its Varying Components

the story between antagonist and protagonist, offering different solutions the protagonist might take by actually getting on stage and performing the suggested alternative, thereby blurring the lines and roles of subject and object, spectator and actor (and in the case of our specific study, teacher educator and teacher). Participants had the power to change situations directly through demonstration and performance. When performing each suggested change, spect-actors came to feel empowered and started conceptualizing themselves as agents—as subjects who could act upon and change oppressive situations, rather than as objectified victims of other people's actions.

Fundamental to Augusto Boal's theatrical process is a mediating party located at the center of the proceedings. This person takes responsibility for the logistical running of the process and ensures a fair proceeding, considering multiple perspectives and/or solutions. One might typically refer to this role as the Facilitator. In Boal's literature, however, this role is referred to as the Joker, in reference to the neutrality of the Joker card in a deck of playing cards. Some of the roles of the Joker, the Facilitator, or the "Difficultator" (Jackson, 1995, p. xix), a term Boal also preferred, include generating participation and recognition of complexity, stimulating reluctant audiences to "difficult-ate" (used as a verb) interventions, working with particular constituencies, and knowing how and when to end a Forum show. Boal typically played the role of the Joker himself, a role of director, facilitator, and critic. After facilitating multiple renderings of the same situation, Boal-the-difficultator asked the spect-actors the question: Is it real? He wanted to challenge and problematize any romanticized or oversimplified solutions that had been offered, and asked: Is the solution presented by the spect-actors possible? If not, then the group would collectively decide to rehearse other possibilities for the future, or, as Boal (1979) stated, engage in a "rehearsal for revolution" (p. 155). This process is explored further in Chapter 5.

THE REVOLUTIONARY NATURE OF BOALIAN THEATRE

As Boal developed T.O. to become a method for rehearsing and carrying out social change, the Brazilian military government began to see Boal and his T.O. practices as a threat. Boal was kidnapped in 1971 as he returned home from the performance of a play he directed. Following this abduction, Boal was exiled, as Freire had been, to other Latin American countries. First exiled to Argentina and then to Peru, Boal later went to Europe. Boal (2005) recounted that Argentina was the birthplace of the Invisible Theatre:

In Argentina I had to do something else, and I like to do theatre in the street. But my friend said don't do theatre in the street because if you got arrested again here in Argentina they're going to send you back to Brazil. And in Brazil they do not arrest the same person twice. The second time they kill directly. So Simona had a good idea, he said, why don't we do the play, but we don't tell anybody that it's a play. So you can be there and no one's responsible for anything because you explode the scene in front of everyone. Everyone can participate. So we did that. We did what they call Invisible Theatre. (¶ 10)

Invisible Theatre emerged to fill the need to continue challenging oppressive situations even in times of censorship. In Invisible Theatre, as people went about their daily lives, issues could be made public. For example, as part of a Freirean literacy program in Peru in the early 1970s, Invisible Theatre was enacted in a public setting—an expensive hotel restaurant. Boal (1979) recounted that a protagonist actor ordered barbecue costing 70 *soles* and voiced his dissatisfaction with the barbecue loudly during the course of his meal. When the check arrived, he said, "I am going to pay for it, but I am broke. . . . So I will pay for it with labor power" (p. 145). He quickly found out (from the head waiter) that he would have to work 10 hours as a garbage thrower in order to pay for the barbecue that took him 10 minutes to eat. Expressing his frustration, he said, "It can't be! Either you increase the salary of the garbage man, or reduce the price of the barbecue" (p. 145). Other actors, sitting at other tables in the same restaurant, engaged in collective dialogue, making visible the exploitation of the poor in affluent settings. In this situation, as in other performances of Invisible Theatre, bystanders would eavesdrop, and although they were not actively participating, they would be forced to think about the social issue being represented. In doing so, Boal found that they would almost always side with the oppressed, not the oppressor. (See Chapter 6 for further discussion of Invisible Theatre.)

During his exile, as Freire had also done, Boal wrote his landmark work concerning social oppression—*Teatro del Oprimido* (1974). The work was subsequently translated into *Theatre of the Oppressed* (1979), a few years after the 1970 publication of *Pedagogy of the Oppressed* by Paulo Freire. Ten years after his exile, during which he continued to teach his liberatory activist theatre throughout the world, Boal orchestrated the first International Festival of the Theatre of the Oppressed in Paris (Campbell, 1995).

In the 1980s, democracy returned to Brazil. A popular movement named *Diretas Já!* (Direct [elections] now!) developed organically and served as a catalyst for change. As part of the Diretas Já! movement, people went to the streets protesting for direct presidential elections, which finally took place in 1989. In the mid-1980s, Boal returned to his native

Rio de Janeiro and was later elected to the office of *vereador* (a full-time, fully funded city council–like position). As vereador, Boal established venues for teaching and performing his theatre, initially relying heavily on two of his most famous techniques: Forum Theatre (previously described) and Image Theatre.

In Boal's Image Theatre, participants are encouraged to use their bodies rather than language to portray and communicate realities. Image Theatre begins with the collective arrangement of bodies in several poses in order to denote a certain prevailing reality—for instance, prejudice. Participants are then asked to portray an ideal image, often without words, by reconfiguring their bodies into living sculptures. In essence, participants are challenged to rethink and redo their realities via body positioning. Boal (1979) proposed that the power of Image Theatre lies in "making thought visible" (p. 137). Image Theatre is explored further in Chapter 4.

While serving as vereador, Boal (1998) established Legislative Theatre using Forum and Image Theatre to generate themes emerging directly from neighborhood and community members to be dealt with in the city council. According to Boal (2001), he employed T.O. as he worked with 19 groups of socioeconomically oppressed citizens. They would perform social problems, discuss those problems with their communities, and dialogue with other communities experiencing similar predicaments. Boal (2001) said:

> Out of these activities many legislative proposals came to my office. We had what we called the metabolizing cell, which was a group of actors and also lawyers. They would transform all the suggestions into proposals for new laws. I would present those proposals in the chamber like any other legislator. But the proposals for legislation would come not out of my head, but from the people. I presented 42 different proposals for new laws, 13 of which were approved. Thirteen laws now in existence in Rio are some of the ones which were proposed by the population (p. 15).

Despite Boal's failed reelection campaign, he continued using Legislative Theatre to raise awareness of local issues in neighborhoods and communities throughout Rio de Janeiro.(See Chapter 6 for further discussion of Legislative Theatre.)

THEATRE OF THE OPPRESSED IN EUROPE, CANADA, AND THE UNITED STATES

Clearly, the many ways to do Boalian Theatre of the Oppressed genuinely serve to envision and enact change. Although much of his work started within the borders of Latin American countries, Boal's theatre techniques had, and continue to have, far-reaching influences in many other continents. Theatre troupes, nursing associations, social workers, educators, and other groups currently employ T.O. across all continents. The list of Theatre of the Oppressed practitioners is inexhaustible, and readers may wish to contact www.ctorio.com.br for an issue of *Metaxis*, which features articles by practitioners worldwide. Those interested in applying T.O. may seek guidance through articles about its use with varied populations (on immigrant students, see Gutiérrez, 2008, and Estrella, Vossoughi, & Espinoza, 2006; on urban youth groups, see Sanders, 2004; on orphans, see Szeman, 2005; on social workers, see Houston, Magill, McCollum, & Spratt, 2001; on the elderly, see Ferrand, 1995, and Schweitzer, 1994; on police recruits, see Telesco & Solomon, 2001; on maximum security prisoners, see Mitchell, 2001; on graduate students of occupational therapy, see Brown & Gillespie, 1997; on resistant writers, see Creel, Kuhne, & Riggle, 2000; on teacher education, see Burgoyne et al., 2005, and Kaye & Ragusa, 1998).

In the United States, T.O. is often referred to by alternative names. This is perhaps reflective of an overall privileged audience not relating to or uncomfortable with the word *oppression*. Or perhaps, as the Mandala Center for Change (2009) in Seattle has written, dropping *oppression* from the title is just "better marketing." In the United States and Canada, "Theatre of the Oppressed" has been called by different names, such as "Theatre of Liberation," "Theatre for Living," and "Redo Theatre" (Mandala Center for Change, 2009). In her theatre work with largely White, middle-class Canadians, Lib Spry (1994) described shifting the language of "oppression" to the language of "liberation," preferring to ask participants who has power-over them rather than who oppresses them:

> By introducing this term "power-over" (Starhawk, 1987: 9) into my TO workshops rather than using the vocabulary of oppression, I have found that people are more prepared to look at the power structures in which they live and the role they play. . . . Understanding these structures is a first step towards change. (pp. 174–175)

In our own work with teachers in the Southeastern United States, we were also ambivalent about using the word *oppressed*. As illustrated by the vignette that begins this chapter, in one of our first workshops Reggie said he wasn't sure he should come because he associated the word *oppressed* with dictatorships in "other," less-developed, more tyrannical countries. Although we believe oppression is located in all sectors of the United States, we chose to label our work as "Creating Multicultural Learning Communities through Theatre," rather than as "Theatre of the Oppressed." We do not want to discourage potential participants who interpret or define oppression more narrowly or geographically, as taking place only in the context of poverty in developing countries. As Boal explained about his experience in democratic France:

> I discovered very soon that I would find in France . . . the same differences that I found in Brazil. In Brazil there are people who are extremely rich among the many millions who are extremely poor . . . in Paris . . . people were oppressed but they had some free time to preoccupy themselves with themselves, with things like solitude, incommunicability, emptiness. I started working on those themes. The *Theatre of the Oppressed* became much more psychological. I started using techniques linked to psychotherapy. When I went back to Brazil in 1986 I started using those techniques there—and they worked. . . . The poor people in the popular schools would never propose such psychotherapeutic work. But if I proposed it they discovered that they had these personal problems too. They don't usually deal with them because the police, money, and boss problems are worse. (In Taussig & Schechner, 1994, p. 26)

During his exile in Paris, Boal (1995) found a very different social consciousness from what he had known in Latin America: "In Latin America, the major killer is hunger; in Europe, it is drug overdose. But, whatever form it comes in, death is still death" (p. 8). Unlike the overt military forces and political dictatorships in developing countries, in more economically advantaged countries such as the United States and France, oppression was more often psychological or covert. This is not to say that there were not psychological forms of oppression in Latin America. Boal observed that in Latin American countries (e.g., Brazil) ruled by military dictatorships, official utterances of the oppressive society had become internalized, silencing emancipatory participation. While the headquarters of the oppression were external, their effect was occurring internally where individuals' own thought processes became a form of self-censorship. This is a complexity that was not articulated so clearly until Boal's later work, *Rainbow of Desire* (Boal, 1995).

Augusto Boal's methods were first explicitly linked to higher education in the United States in 1992 when he was a keynote speaker for the National Conference of the Association of Theatre in Higher Education. This was the year in which Boal's *Games for Actors and Non-Actors* was published (first in French, then translated to English), and became a must-read for those already using T.O. This book provided a thorough and theoretically sound introduction for those new to T.O., the "non-actors," along with methods, techniques, games, and exercises that are simple to use. In this book, Boal presented theatre as social therapy, as a way to "dismantle social masks and rituals" (p. 191) by offering new perspectives on old, oppressive, and recurring situations.

Even though Boal did not write at length about the importance of games for rehearsing the revolution until the 1990s, theatre games have always served as a critical foundation for his work, enabling spectactors to practice the play of physical revolution (see also Chapter 3). According to Boal (1979), because we are so conditioned to and rely so heavily on expressing ourselves verbally, our bodies' expressive capabilities remain underdeveloped. Exercises presented by Boal (1992) are designed to "undo," or demechanize, the participants' physical ways of reacting to situations and being in the world, changing a person's muscular habits while raising consciousness about how one's body structure is representative of an idea, situation, or way of being.

In 1995, Boal published *The Rainbow of Desire*, which elaborated on therapeutic applications of Boalian theatre. In the book, Boal further refined his definitions of oppression to include the "Cop in the Head" (p. 40), the internalized voice(s) of oppression that prevent(s) one from living fully. Rainbow of Desire techniques explore the tensions, fears, and desires of people in relationships, informing moment-to-moment interaction. (See Chapter 6 for further discussion of Rainbow of Desire.)

Rainbow of Desire introduces a kind of carnivalesque performance, not unlike that addressed by Bakhtin (1984) in *Rabelais and His World*. Although each has a different emphasis, both Bakhtin's carnival and Boal's Rainbow of Desire capture the dialogic interrelationship of power as expressed through a complex unity of varied utterances. Boal's Rainbow of Desire techniques allow spectactors to explore the partiality of their subject positions, to understand that one can simultaneously occupy the position of oppressor and oppressed, thereby addressing one of the major critiques of Paulo Freire's work and of critical pedagogy. Rainbow of Desire techniques were designed for the context of economically advanced countries where individuals' psychosocial oppressions often stem from a carnival of competing, often contradictory, desires to be efficient, machine-like, and objective, yet inefficient, subjective, and, in essence, human. Yet as explained above, this technique also strengthened Boal's work and applications in Latin America.

Until his death on May 2, 2009, 12 years to the day after Freire, Boal continued to conduct workshops on T.O. We dedicate this book to honor the profound influence that Augusto Boal's texts, teachings, and person have had on our own work in education, and we hope this book will help others carry on his important legacy.

Teachers Act Up!
Practicing Transformative Theatre

THE CHAPTERS IN this part are devoted to exploring the dimensions and details of the Boalian techniques introduced in Chapter 2. We focus on specific cases of teacher struggle and what these performed struggles reveal
about the potential for teachers as change agents in their own lives and
the lives of their students.

Chapter 3 provides a review of "games" accompanied by photographic
images and easy-to-follow descriptions (which we refer to as Joker's Rules)
of how the games may be led. Based on the assumption that one must
undo the body's habits and movements in order to challenge status quo
ways of thinking and being in the world, this chapter explores the importance of developing body awareness through creative, physical activity
within a group.

Chapter 4 continues to develop understandings of Boal's games, adding Image Theatre exercises, which focus on various kinds of embodied
sculpture activities and the profound physical and psychic impact nonverbal

activities have on the spect-actor. Through the use of bodies as sculptural "clay," participants can create images that reflect their perception of a situation or perspective in the world. Photos and explanations of how to engage in Image Theatre are also included.

Moving from discrete games and image work, Chapters 5 and 6 develop longer narrative scripts that illuminate tensions in teachers' lived experiences. Chapter 5 focuses on Forum Theatre, which elicits three-part narrative structures detailing dramatic tensions between Protagonist teachers and Antagonist interlocutors, including administrators, students, colleagues, paraprofessionals, parents, and professors. Again, photographic images are used to share the sequence of these "no-budget" productions accompanied by "trans/scripts"—actual written and dramatized transcripts from our performance work with teachers (Cahnmann-Taylor, Wooten, Souto-Manning, & Dice, 2009).

Rainbow of Desire, one of Boal's (1995) most recently developed techniques, is introduced in Chapter 6. Moving from one Protagonist and one Antagonist, teachers explore the multivocality of a single individual and the various motivations behind one's spoken words and actions. Rainbow of Desire allows spect-actors to explore the partiality of their subject positions, to understand that one can simultaneously occupy the positions of oppressor and oppressed. Also reviewed in Chapter 6 are Invisible Theatre and Legislative Theatre.

Liberating the Body: More Than Fun in Games

TO MAINTAIN the energy and passion that drive many men and women to enter the teaching profession, more opportunities to play are needed in order to release stress and rehearse change. After all, according to Plato, "You can discover more about a person in an hour of play than in a year of conversation." As a result, it is important that teachers and teacher educators engage in exploring and practicing the mysteries of play. But how do we invite play into educational spaces that are otherwise occupied by the intellectual, rational, disembodied, and scientific? Within the many pressures to acquire evidence-based practices and precise teaching methods that will ensure students' speedy acquisition of literacy and test score gains, where is there room for struggle, self-questioning, spontaneity, and restless, embodied innovation?

Spanish Civil War poet Federico Garcia Lorca's answer was to invoke what he called the *duende*, "an emotive and poetic logic rather than a disembodied rational logic" (Hirsch, 1999, p. 13). Duende's etymological root comes from *duen de casa*, "master of the house," a house that is filled with emotion and death. Like the flamenco singer or bullfighter whose dark improvisational arts place them closer to death, duende allows one to succumb to mystery, and absorb its carnival of hunger, desire, sin, and sunlight.

In our work as teacher educators, our goal has been to find innovative and embodied ways to prepare teachers to engage in play regarding the mystery of the unknown. Despite numerous pressures for teachers to know, drill, test, and report, we aim to access the place where spontaneity and creativity join, resulting in new ideas being actualized into reality (Moreno, 1978; Sternberg & Garcia, 2000). We propose that teachers can creatively find possibilities for change as they engage in play.

Barker (1983/1977) bemoaned the fact that adults have lost so much of the mystery and varied movement they once had as exploratory children, having atrophied or lost mind-body skills for creative ways of being in the world. According to Barker:

> Through games, the child explores the range of movement possibilities open to him. . . . Later, in response to personal, parental, and social pressures, he selects those skills and movement patterns which he thinks will best express his purposes in life, or which suit the persona he conceives will best present himself to the world. What is clear is that by adolescence the child has lost many of the skills which he had at an earlier age. . . . Like all learning processes, it is liable to inhibition at various stages. (p. 63)

Likewise, Boal (1992) believed that we too quickly fall into "mechanized" ways of being in our bodies, automating muscle structures and habits, preventing ourselves from perceiving varied emotions and sensations. Why is it that some of us are accustomed to walking with our chests out, gaze forward; others with shoulders sunk and eyes downcast? What about ourselves do we change when we tiptoe away from a sleeping baby or charge down a school corridor to separate two students in a fistfight? Boal suggested that we examine our physical habits and their contexts, exploring how expanded repertoires for the presentation of oneself (Goffman, 1959) affect possibilities for personal and social emancipation.

Boal believed there were social consequences for those who are stuck in the mechanized habits of the body, trapping an individual into a predetermined role and limiting one's possibilities to create individual and social change. To demechanize the body is to awaken one's awareness of muscular potential, the relationship between self and other, and our capacity to restructure our expressive and communicative potential. "Games," "Exercises," or "gamesercises" (Boal, 1992, p. 60) offer opportunities to become more conscious of our bodies and minds, our relationships between how we physically carry ourselves in the world and our abilities to perceive ourselves as doers, agents of change.

This chapter is about how teachers and teacher educators can use a varied "arsenal" (Boal, 1992) of theatre games to raise body-mind awareness, rehearsing multifaceted and improvisational ways of being and thinking in the world. As in most, if not all, Boalian workshops as well as many theatre workshops in general, we begin each performance-based workshop with warm-up games. These games may be as playful as variations on childhood games such as pin the tail on the donkey or a potato sack race. There are numerous theatre books that describe a wide variety of games to stretch both the body and mind's imagination and potential for play (c.f., Barker, 1983/1977; Heathcote & Bolton, 1995; Lobman & Lundquist, 2007; Rohd, 1998; Saldaña, 1995; Spolin, 1999; Sternberg & Garcia, 2000). However, our purpose has always been twofold. More than just fun and games, we aim for each exercise to work on a physical as well as conceptual level. We have chosen to implement and share games whose metaphorical power ignites important questions related to teaching:

- Who is in charge?
- What is the purpose of education?
- How is language learned and taught?
- How are inequalities perpetuated, and what is the role of education in furthering or curtailing unfair distributions of resources?

We begin the following section with an explanation of the basic rules for the games described in this chapter and the image exercises in Chapter 5. Then we present an easy-to-follow guide for our selection of games. In this way, readers can learn from and build on our experience of using gaming techniques and do what all great teachers do: beg, borrow, and steal ideas and then adapt these treasures to one's own needs in one's own context. We hope that by focusing on "thick description" (Geertz, 1973) of a selection of games we've used with pre- and in-service teachers, readers will come away with a clear understanding of a variety of gaming techniques and their metaphorical power for expanding teacher dialogue, which has the potential to lead to transformation.

ESTABLISHING GROUND RULES

As explained in Chapter 2, Boal gave the name "Joker" to the facilitator (or "difficultator," as Boal defined this role). The Joker is the person in charge, reminding participants of the rules negotiated. The Joker walks a fine line, as she is situated both as one who is neutral, like the Joker in a deck of cards, but also as one who establishes guidelines and takes responsibility for facilitating the interactions and re-enactments that will take place. The Joker constantly engages in dialectically negotiating (and re-negotiating) authority. We acknowledge the complexities of "playing" the Joker, as some believe Jokers should never participate in the spect-acting process while others disagree (Schutzman & Cohen-Cruz, 1994). We have thought long and hard, continuously and recursively, about what the Joker can do and how to play the Joker. We have decided that this is context dependent. Occasionally, we decided to play the Joker as a spect-actor, as we saw our role in a very Freirean sense (Freire, 1998b), as blurred, learning alongside our participants in the process of facilitating the Acting Up! workshops.

Since the games we play can often expose participants to physical and/ or emotional vulnerability, it is important to prepare them through an opening agenda and to structure games to build trust and a sense of community. When asked to play a game, young people and adults alike want to know the rules. For that reason, we begin each session with five basic ground rules. Like all good teachers, we know that these rules are likely to shift, expanding and/or contracting according to the needs of the group.

Basic Ground Rules

1. Take an oath of confidentiality.
2. Share the conversational floor.
3. Listen for understanding, not rebuttal.
4. Play within the parameters of your own body.
5. Make the experience new.

We ask each person in the room to take an oath of confidentiality, meaning that what is shared during the session with one another will not be shared outside the confines of the room. Cultivating a sense of trust relies on a commitment to protect one another's right to anonymity and freedom to share openly without fear of public exposure. We also ask each participant to be aware of what linguists have referred to as "the conversational floor" (Edelsky, 1981), being mindful of turn-taking, and to collectively aim to hear as many voices as possible. While many of the Boalian activities are to be done in silence, these are often followed by group dialogue. Thus, we remind participants to be aware of each person's comfort level with talking in front of a group and that, as teachers, we want to work consciously on ways to elicit as much participation as possible from each member. Building upon conscious speaking, we also encourage participants to be conscious of listening—to be attentive to understanding what is being said rather than listening in order to formulate a rebuttal to what has been said.

Given that much of the game activity involves considerable physical movement, our fourth rule asks that everyone play within the parameters of his or her own body. What is a simple movement for one person may be physically demanding for another. We encourage participants to tailor all instructions to their own ability and comfort level without any fear that their participation will be considered incomplete. In partner games, one might have to communicate one's needs in creative ways—especially when working in nonverbal structures. Gazes, gestures, freezes—there are many ways to communicate one's limits. While respecting that all bodies' needs and abilities differ, we also ask participants to think of their bodies as "an undiscovered country rather than a mountainous barrier; a mine of untapped resources rather than an arid landscape" (Barker, 1983/1977, p. 97). We select games that may stretch one's perceived limitations and encourage safe exploration of one's boundaries.

Finally, we ask each participant to make the experience new. Some participants have played the same games in multiple workshops with us or with other Boalian Jokers in distant settings. We believe that these games are designed so that each person can repeat an exercise multiple times and still come away with something new. Even as teachers engage in the same kinds of activities, we have found that interactional and/or temporal contexts influence the result of the experience. Participants consider the activities in light of new contexts and components.

As teacher educators, we also come away with new learnings and understandings from each experience. We ask how one might play any particular game differently from before? We realize that each teacher's experiences, expectations, cultural practices, and background knowledge, as well as the collective experiences and dynamics, influence understandings and interpretations of the game activities. Together with participating teachers, we examine the issues involved in coming to gaming and all creative activity as different persons from who we were before. We consider ways in which we could encounter what we have/had already experienced in a new way.

Here, we propose that identifying one's own personal learning edge will be important for any teacher or teacher educator who wants to keep the "same material" (read content and standards) new for all students, while cultivating students' sense of ownership and valuing their situated experiences. Therefore, we invite players to participate in demechanizing their bodies, considering multiple perspectives. As we are about to start, we ask: What do *you* want to learn from this exercise today?

THE GAMES

In this chapter we introduce six games, each with a multitude of extensions and variations. We provide guidance regarding the optimum number of players and approximate duration, and we expect readers to try out their own variations with their own communities (and we hope you'll tell us about it!). Each game is introduced by a short description and goals to help the reader understand our intentions as teacher educators, and each includes a set of "Joker's Rules" laying out how to guide participants through these exercises. We have borrowed instructions from theatre teachers and writers with whom we have worked and/or whose texts we have studied. Examples from play and/or teachers' reflections and discussions are included at the end of the exercise. We hope these examples, along with the accompanying photos, will help readers feel as if they were with us in the room, and be able to transform the games to use in a new context.

WHAT'S IN A NAME?

Number of people: 5–25 (higher numbers are possible but may prove
    exhausting)
Time: 5–20 minutes

Short Description and Goals: No one wants to be referred to as "Hey you!," but this game offers more than a clever way to learn individual names. Beyond just learning one another's names, this game incorporates rhythm, sound, and play as a strong foundation for developing a sense of creative spontaneity and community. Warming up, participants learn to embody their companions' names, words, movements, and identities, and in this way, add to their muscular repertoires. Name games may bear repeating, especially if new members join the same group or if significant time passes between sessions. If everyone already knows one another's names, we suggest variations below that can still make use of this energizing way to start.

Joker's Rules

1. With everyone standing in a circle, demonstrate the game action by saying your name and one thing that describes you, and make a simultaneous movement to accompany the name/adjective pair.

2. Ask the person on the right to do the same and so on around the circle.
3. Encourage participants to spontaneously use an adjective that starts with the same letter of their name or rhymes with their name.
4. Encourage participants to exaggerate their movements, making themselves bigger or smaller than they might otherwise be in daily life. As Boal (1992, p. 88) wrote, "If everybody is ridiculous, no one is!"
5. After each contribution, ask the group to echo the name/adjective/ movement combination, making an exact mirror of the speaker— masculine or feminine, Latino or White, Spanish or English, and so forth. This is not a caricature, but a restructuring of our own ways of being to gain a better sense of the interior of the other person (Boal, 1992).
6. Acting as a conductor, lead the entire group to chant each name/ adjective/movement, cycling back from the beginning, creating a form of repetitive group poem (see Figure 3.1).

Example

PERSON ONE: "Mama Misha" (*said in a cooing manner while cradling a small make-believe baby in her arms*).

Figure 3.1. What's in a Name?

EVERYONE: "Mama Misha" (*said in a cooing manner while participants cradle small make-believe babies in their arms*).

PERSON TWO: "Esperanza Danza" (*said while twisting her hips and waving hands in the air*).

EVERYONE: "Mama Misha" (*said in a cooing manner while participants cradle a small make-believe baby in their arms*); "Esperanza Danza" (*said while participants twist their hips and wave their hands in the air*).

PERSON THREE: "Multitasking Mariana" (*said in an urgent and frantic manner while trying to reach in four or five directions simultaneously*).

EVERYONE: "Mama Misha" (*said in a cooing manner while participants cradle a small make-believe baby in their arms*); "Esperanza Danza" (*said while participants twist their hips and wave their hands in the air*); "Multitasking Mariana" (*said in an urgent and frantic manner while participants try to reach in four or five directions simultaneously*).

And so on.

Extensions

- At the end, ask if someone can chant all the name/adjective/movement combos alone.
- Ask individuals to change places with one another in the circle and try to repeat the "poem" in its new order.

Variations

- Ask participants to say their name and also state their mood in terms of a color (e.g., "Maroon Misha").
- Use a ball or beanbag and have participants toss it across the circle and say hello to the receiver (e.g., Misha tosses to Esperanza and says, "Hola, Esperanza Danza!").
- If participants already know one another's names, a short variation is to simply say one's name with an exaggerated action and ask the group to mirror the action/name back.
- If participants already know one another's names or wear visible nametags, ask a participant to come to the center and call out another person's name three times. To remain in the circle, a call-ee has to say his or her own name before the caller has finished the name in triple. Otherwise, the call-ee goes to the center. (Thanks to Julian Boal for that last variation!)

Example

DEBORA: (*in the center calls*) Misha, Misha, //Misha.
MISHA: //Misha! (*Misha keeps her place*)
DEBORA: (*in the center calls*) David, David, David
DAVID: Uh-oh. (*changes places with Debora*)

Note: // indicates overlapping speech.

HOW MANY A'S IN AN A?

Number of people: 5–25
Time: 5–20 minutes

Short Description and Goals: As with the name game, this game is designed so that participants engage in reproducing another member's way of speaking, moving, and being in the world, while rehearsing endless variations. A good, quick warm-up, this exercise reinforces creativity, spontaneity, and playfulness in the group. Used with students from preschool to adulthood, this activity reminds us of our vast and varied communicative potential, without using any "real words" at all.

Joker's Rules

1. Have the participants stand in a circle.
2. Ask them to think of a feeling, emotion, or idea that they can express using only the sound of the letter "A," interpreted in any way they like (e.g., "a" as in *late, bat, father,* or as spoken in another language).
3. As one participant after another offers his or her interpretation, lead the group members to echo all the sounds and actions.
4. Again, encourage big actions and exaggerated sounds (see Figure 3.2).

Example 1

"Ah ah ah" ("ah" as in "father" said in a warning manner while waving one's finger in the air as if to say "no no no.")

Example 2

"Eyyyyyyyyy" ("ey" as in "late" said with exaggerated smile and hip swagger, thumb up, and knee forward).

Figure 3.2. How Many A's in an A?

Variations

- Repeat the same activity, going through other vowels: E, I, O, U.
- Participants may explore variations on a single word or sentence rather than just a single vowel sound—e.g., how many different sounds and actions might correspond with the word *teacher* or often-repeated sentences such as "Please pay attention" or "Open your books"?

Participants' Reflections: In follow-up dialogue, many teachers reflected on this game as a way to create community, foster trust, and to get to know each other's names.

STOPPING AROUND

Number of people: Any number
Time: 10–20 minutes

Short Description and Goals: This game is designed so participants experience the unexpected—rules and expectations turned upside-down. Participants listen to words that mean one thing and are asked to do something else, heightening attention to connections between language and meaning. During this activity, participants have opportunities to prepare their bodies to move away from expected reactions toward specific situations or stresses. They start considering what verbal directions mean as they think in order to act as opposed to acting a certain way on impulse. In addition, participants consider the implications of teaching and learning in ways that are unexpected, breaking with social convention.

Joker's Rules

1. Ask participants to walk around the room.
2. Call "STOP!" Participants stop.
3. Call "WALK!" Participants walk.
4. Add Complication #1: Ask participants to walk when they hear "stop" and stop when they hear "walk." Give a few minutes of rehearsal; then yell "walk" and all freeze in their places.
5. Add Complication #2: Ask participants to jump when they hear "name" and to shout their name when they hear "jump."
6. Add Complication #3: Ask participants to put their hands in the air when they hear "knees" and to put hands on their knees when they hear "hands."
7. Call any one of these commands in quick and varied succession.

Example

Joker calls out:

Stop! (*all participants walk around the room at a leisurely pace*).
Walk! (*participants stop*).
Stop! (*participants walk*).
Jump! (*all participants shout their names and continue walking*).
Knees! (*participants wave hands in the air and continue walking*).
Name! (*participants jump, then continue walking*).

Note: *Many participants will become confused; there will be a great deal of laughter. While engaging in this game, participants will become more aware of their bodies and body movements.*

Variations

- Repeat the same activity, using any additional pairs of commands, e.g., quiet/noise, (walk on your) tiptoes/heels, sing/moan, and so on.

- Include trios instead of pairs of interchangeable commands—e.g., "walk," "stop," and "jump" to mean "jump," "walk," and "stop," respectively. Introduce new trios as needed or wanted.

Participants' Reflections: In follow-up dialogue, many teachers reflected on this game as applied to classroom practice.

> ANGELA: As a foreign language teacher, I use this game in the second language, calling out instructions and then checking for understanding while having fun. If I say *"nombre"* (name) and that actually means *"brincar"* (jump), then it really checks for their understanding of vocabulary in an engaging way!
>
> MARLENA: In elementary grades, children often have trouble with following directions, especially with the kindergarten, first-, and second-graders. So this is a good way students can practice listening to and following directions while having fun, too!

HOUSE, INHABITANT, TEMPEST

Number of people: Minimum of 12 preferred
Time: 5–20 minutes

Short Description and Goals: As so much of teaching requires spontaneity and accommodating the materials at hand, this game provides a joyful rehearsal of the chaos and confusion that often accompany creative classroom activity. The game also introduces the idea of people working and playing together to achieve a common goal within constrained conditions. Although these could not be attained alone, collectiveness makes it possible.

Joker's Rules

1. Divide participants into groups of three. In each group two participants face one another, standing a foot or 2 apart, raising and linking their hands to form the "roof" of a house. The third participant, the "inhabitant," stands inside this newly created "house" (see Figure 3.3). (This physical positioning appears to be a variation on the children's game London Bridge).
2. Call out "inhabitant." Then all inhabitants must vacate their house and run to another.

Figure 3.3. House, Inhabitant, Tempest

3. Call out "house." Then the inhabitants remain still, while the participants forming houses must separate and find a new partner with whom to form a new house over a new inhabitant.
4. Call out "tempest." Someone who was previously a "house" can decide to remain a house or change to become an inhabitant. Then chaos reigns, and everybody moves, changing roles, choosing either to be a house or inhabitant.
5. If the number of players is not divisible by 3, the player who finds her/himself outside the house/inhabitant groups of three can call out the category instead of the Joker.

Example

JOKER: Inhabitant please, Inhabitant!

Inhabitants start to search for new homes, participants who are "houses" start to make comments such as "Come into our home," "Welcome to our humble abode." Participants are actively running around the room looking for a "house."

Joker: We've got all of this prime real estate here!

(Joker gestures toward the center of the room (all of the "houses" and "inhabitants" are along the sides of the room).

Joker: Okay, House!

The "houses" separate and seek new partners. A new "house" partnership shouts, "We need an inhabitant!" Group laughter as they run together to cover a new "inhabitant."

Joker: Tempest!

All participants storm around the room to find new places as either a "house" or an "inhabitant." Much laughter ensues. Participants ask the Joker, "We can become anything?" They ask each other, "Can I be your house?" and "May I be your inhabitant?"

Variations

- Have more than one "inhabitant" per "house"—ask houses to set the "stage," opening their roofs and making room for two! This is a particularly useful variation when working with a number of participants indivisible by 3.
- Choose one "inhabitant" to be "A," the other, "B." "A" wants to leave the house; "B" wants "A" to stay. Ask inhabitants to immediately play a short improvisational dialogue based on their distinct motivations. The houses may also become animated and take sides—either assisting or preventing A in departure.

  a. One pair will be selected to perform a conflict in the middle of the room for the whole group.
  b. Another option is to break into groups and have several renderings of this struggle being performed concurrently (Rohd, 1998).

Participants' Reflections: In follow-up reflections and interviews, many teachers discussed the power and possibilities of this game:

Fernanda: This game opens us up to the fact that there are all these unsafe places. But that's okay, as a teacher (or as a student) you can just open yourself up and get used to the fact that you're going to be moving around, you're going to be looking for people to work with, and it's okay—you're going to find a house eventually or you're going to *be* a house!

DENISE: I think it's interesting because it seemed like everyone wanted to be the house. Maybe because it was easy to recognize somebody else who wanted to be a house and we are always looking for that structure.

FERNANDA: As teachers, we're all part of putting the house together, that's what I say in the classroom. Together we create the structures and together we can break them.

POWER SHUFFLE

Number of people: Minimum of 8–10; can be adapted to a larger number of participants

Time: 10–40 minutes

Short Description and Goals: This exercise, designed by Marc Weinblatt (2006), is a variation of a sociodramatic technique called The Line Up (Sternberg & Garcia, 2000, p. 242), in which group members arrange themselves in a continuum based on various categories, such as height, date of birth, length of time in the United States, and so forth. Power Shuffle adds the dimension of power by asking participants to leave the safety of one line and expose levels of power and privilege in the group. This game challenges the good intentions many teachers have to see all students as the same, regardless of differences in race, class, gender, parents' educational background, etc. This colorblind and difference-blind orientation overlooks important historical and social differences that place unfair obstacles and burdens on some more than others. This game requires a sense of group trust and may be most productive after participants have had a chance to get to know one another.

Joker's Rules

1. Ask participants to stand in one line across one side of a cleared space in the room.
2. Call out a category (see examples of dominant categories in Figure 3.4). Tell participants that if they fit within the category called, they should cross to the other side of the room. Do not explain categories, and encourage participants to make their own judgments regarding whether they fit the category or not and where to stand.

---

1. Aged 21–59
2. A man
3. Ablebodied
4. Raised in a Christian household
5. White/Euro-American
6. United States born/U.S. citizen
7. Heterosexual
8. Raised middle-class (enough or more than enough resources)
9. ("Standard") English as the first language

Figure 3.4. Some Dominant Categories We've Used

3. Once each crossing is complete, say to participants, "Notice who's with you, who's not with you. How do you feel?" (see Figure 3.5).
4. Then have all return to the starting line, and call another category.

Example

JOKER: If you are a man, please cross to the other side of the room.

In silence, participants cross to the other side of the room based on their own judgment and belief as to whether or not they belong to the specific category.

JOKER: Look around. Notice who is with you, who's not with you. How do you feel?

These questions are not yet to be answered, as dialogue occurs at the game's conclusion.

Discussion: After the activity is complete, ask pairs or small groups to sit and share their experience of this exercise. Then engage in group dialogue, introducing the terms *Target* and *Agent*.

Targets. Individuals who don't fit any given dominant categories can be targets of oppression. Targets are members of social identity groups that are disenfranchised, exploited, and/or victimized in varying ways by institutions and society as a whole. Targets can simultaneously be or become Agents in powerful and/or destructive ways.

Figure 3.5. Power Shuffle

Agents. Agents are members of dominant groups with many unearned, unwanted, and/or unconscious privileges, power, and access within institutions and society as a whole. Shame often comes up for Agents and can be paralyzing, preventing action. Agents can exploit their agency and/or potentially become powerful allies of Targets.

Extension: Ask participants to cluster in groups of three or four around a shared identity as an "Agent" where privilege is a concern to them (e.g., concern about economic privilege, racial privilege, religious privilege, etc.). Using each others' bodies, sculpt an image of what this privilege/agency looks and feels like to members in the group. Each group will provide a title and share their image with the larger group for discussion.

Participants' Reflections: Below, participants offered their perspectives as they reflected on the Power Shuffle activity in light of their own teaching, context, and students (Carla). Participants started questioning what is middle-class (David), the concept of middle-class across borders—what is perceived to be middle-class in one country might equal the concept of poverty in another (Boyang). Likewise, participants questioned what it means to be White across international contexts.

CARLA: We have to get our students to accept themselves and accept who they are, to be able to feel relaxed in a classroom. It doesn't make any sense to pretend everybody's White or heterosexual. Because we are not. We are all different. I like this activity very much, because I think it helps us fight against inhibition.

DAVID: A lot of times, like when you asked some of the questions, for example, "Do you feel you had enough or more than enough resources," I didn't know how to respond. It's the way you perceive yourself. Because I, for one, have no idea how much my parents make; that's something they don't share with me. So how do I know for sure? I don't. I know they give me certain things. And I'm comfortable saying I'm middle-class. Why? Because I'm not Bill Gates. I just think unless you define everything, everyone's thinking their own thing. So you don't know for sure, but it made me think.

BOYANG: What's the standard? When I was growing up, Korea was a really poor country and even if I grew up in a "middle-class" home, which I did most of the time, I didn't do everything I wanted to. . . . Middle-class people here in the United States had more opportunities and so I didn't cross [when that category was called].

CARMELITA: Who's White? Who is White? Am I White? Just the European people, the American people? Latin Americans, I'm from Colombia, are we White?

In the Power Shuffle activity, participants start noticing privileges and talking about differences and discomforts. Because the process of crossing the room, or not, may make participants very uncomfortable, post-game discussion is key. Nevertheless, we propose that it is important to become aware of the visible, less visible, or invisible border crossings that people negotiate day in and day out and believe that this is a good way to start recognizing and naming the issues.

CARNIVAL

Number of people: Minimum of 15 (multiples of 3 preferred)
Time: 10–40 minutes

Short Description and Goals: This game explores issues of assimilation, power, erasure, domination, persuasion, and influence. It is a visual re-minder of how some individuals have the power to persuade others to engage in a certain activity (or believe something) even if they initially espouse another perspective. It also makes visible the tendency to assimilate and replace one's beliefs, actions, and ways of being in the process of trying to belong. In Carnival, groups start with different actions and sounds and try to persuade others to join in (or buy into) the specific behavior. Each group member attempts to get others to behave the way he or she does, leaving aside their original practices. This mirrors the process through which many immigrants assimilate, transforming or erasing their perspectives and cultural practices.

Joker's Rules

1. Have participants form groups of three and number themselves "1," "2," and "3."
2. Ask each individual to come up with a sound and an accompanying movement and teach them to the other two group members.
3. Call out "Number Ones!" and instruct the "1s" to perform their sound and movement, with the other members trying to make an exact imitation.
4. Call out "Number Twos!" for the "2s" to perform, and the others to imitate and learn.
5. Call "Number Threes!" for the "3s" to perform, and the others to imitate and learn.
6. Call out "Original Movements!" and ask 1s, 2s, and 3s all to perform their own separate movements simultaneously.
7. Call out "Unify!" and ask each group member to try to get the other two to adopt his or her sound and movement (see Figure 3.6).
8. When each trio has unified and found a group sound and movement, call out "Groups Unify!" Each trio moves as a pod and aims to attract members of other pods to adopt their sound and movement. The object is to find out which sound/movement will unify (or dominate) the group.

Variations

- When groups initially try to unify within their first trio, announce, "You may change groups—if you're happy, stay put; if you want to change, change" (Boal, 1992, p. 98). Anyone left by him- or herself must join another group.
- Start with the same sound and movement and have groups introduce slight (or dramatic) changes and try to convince the entire group to collaborate.

Figure 3.6. Carnival

Discussion: How is what we did a metaphor for race, class, and culture?

Participants' Reflections: Reflecting on the activity and the discussion that ensued, participants voiced direct connections between this exercise and their experiences as newcomers in different social contexts. Some of the most common themes related to immigration that were expressed by participants are listed below:

- Dominant culture and the cost of assimilation
- Violent coercion
- Marginalization
- "You're either with us or against us" mentality
- Weakened resistance

LEARNING CASE

In the case presented below, pre-service and in-service teachers explored ways in which complex concepts such as the status of English, assimilation, and Whiteness were discussed after the game Carnival. These are difficult topics to tackle, yet games are a wonderful way to explore the complexities and tensions involved. As you read the learning case below, we invite you to jot down some notes about how you think you might employ this game in your own setting.

> We have several groups playing the game, each performing their "unified" sound/action, including clapping rhythmically, a chorus of "Yoo-hoo," and arms thrown in the air above heads, bodies twirling in a circle with the index finger in the air, and a sort of jig. Each group initially resists giving up their sound/action, and as time goes on, some members become even more emphatic about their sound/action, such as an extra boisterous "Yoo-hoo!"
>
> Before long, most of the group adopts the hand clapping, though one person sticks to a loud and enthusiastic "Yoo-hoo!" and ultimately gives up. Two other holdouts maintain their hip wiggle over the clapping. They, too, begin clapping but maintain a rhythmic hip swing. Catherine, the player who first led the hand clapping, shouts "Yee-haw," because by this time, everyone is doing the same action. The game ends, and discussion begins:
>
> JOKER (*seated on the floor with all of the participants in a circle*): I would like to hear your impressions of what happened, and particularly as a metaphor for power, for language, race, class, issues of power.
>
> MARISOL (*clapping*): Go, Girl power! Girl power! She's [Catherine] a strong leader and she's not gonna stop until she wins!
>
> JOKER: Apart from her as an individual, can you extrapolate what this might mean in society, how this exercise might become a metaphor for social interaction?
>
> MARISOL: Well, for a while I wasn't going to give up my own movement, and then José's like "C'mon, let's clap" (*begins to clap*). I just went, "All right. Let's get this done" (*shrugs her shoulders, looking defeated*).
>
> AMANDA: I think we followed the claps because everybody already knew how to clap, and we were supposed to be in a carnival. We didn't need to talk in order to follow the clap. The other movements, you'd need to explain something, or pay more attention.
>
> ANA: Well, for me, I was just kinda dizzy twirling, and as I was getting dizzy, and I said, "Hmm, that works better"; you know, it was more a practical kind of thing.

NELLY: In terms of a social metaphor, we have to adapt to the
environment that we're in. If we're in the United States and
they speak English, we gotta learn to speak English. It's like
over here, we're in a group, and, you know, we had to adapt
to the other people in order for us to agree.

ROSA: As someone who grew up bilingual, it wasn't hard for me to
keep up my Spanish, but for me to teach my *children* Spanish,
it's just a little too hard; it's just a lot easier to completely
assimilate, bring them up speaking English because to teach
'em Spanish would take a *whole* lot more effort.

MARCIA: I was thinking about the kids in my class. Sometimes it
just gets tiring to be different, and they want to assimilate, and
it's really sad because they're losing a part of their heritage
because they're not willing to fight for it or don't think it's
important enough to fight for, even.

MARISOL: Well, I feel like I've assimilated, and I don't feel like I've
lost *any* part that I didn't want to lose; I mean, it's just how it's
happened. I don't think that I've made a conscious decision. As
I grew up, my parents would say "Oh, *estás americanizando"*—
you've Americanized yourself. I'm like, yeah, some things are
really *good* about the American culture! I feel like the more
international I can be, the more I can pick and choose and
become a better person. So I don't feel that I've lost anything I
didn't want to lose (*shrugs her shoulders*). Even in the game, we
weren't just clapping. In our first little group of three, everyone pretty much was doing a little dance. There was a little
Caribbean thing going on. When we were the group of three
doing our little clap, I, we all just kinda started bouncing too
(*starts to bounce where she sits*), didn't we? I think that made it
work better. It wasn't just the clap. It was the clap *and* the
Caribbean dance.

MADALENA: I realized that everybody was doing the same thing so I
did the same thing. At first, I tried not to. But you said, "Try to
convince them, the others," and I said, "Well, how am I going
to convince the others to do what I'm doing?" So, I just *kept* on
doing what I was *doing*, but at the end, well, I saw everybody
was clapping, so let's clap (*raises both hands up as if in defeat*).

CATHERINE: This is a lesson! You can look at it in so many ways.
You can learn, not only in terms of culture, but also with your
children and students. I mean there are *so many* things that this
particular game implies and it *is* easy to get people to come
over to your side, you know. And sometimes I *hope* that you

don't let the, I'll call us gringos, my people, jump in to *your* styles if you're from another country or heritage. I hope that you wouldn't let us take over or take away, but like Marisol said, she's keeping her language and culture going too, which is good, you know.

ROSA: I think this game would be great with kids, especially around those in the late elementary years and that middle school period when what they want more than *anything* is to be *just* like everybody else. You know, they have to buy their clothes at a certain place and do their hair a certain way. So, I see *them* as being very *swayable*, and so it would be an interesting activity.

The Carnival game illustrates and helps name the processes of assimilation, of domination, and persuasion. The discussion that ensues, such as that above, is extremely important, as it problematizes the process illuminated by the game. While the game allows participants to make such processes visible, the dialogue enables participants to extrapolate the experience, applying it to other contexts.

GAMES AS REHEARSALS FOR CHANGE

Overall, games are a powerful way to get started, to warm up the body. They allocate time and space to demechanize our bodies and rethink ways of being in the world. Through games, participants activate and connect their physical bodies in fun and creative, even unusual ways. Most important, such games allow for the body to engage in nonroutine, unknown movements, providing the sensation that we are stepping outside our own bodies. Games allow us to start understanding social reality and our roles in it. In doing so, we can start thinking about, rehearsing, and enacting different ways of acting, reacting, and being. Boal proposed that by understanding social reality and by demechanizing our physical and mental actions, we can begin to change our realities.

Seeing Is Believing:
Image Theatre Is Worth a Thousand Words

[Images] are the "pictures" of the written word. You will likely remember an old Chinese proverb: "A picture is worth a thousand words." If you do, your recollection would not be correct. That statement is a misinterpretation of the original proverb, which actually stated: "A picture's meaning can express ten thousand words," the latter interpretation providing a better balance between the value of pictures and words. But as stated either way, the proverb provides a powerful analogy that can be applied to both the written and spoken word.

—WT Subalusky, *The Observant Eye*

CONSIDERING THE POWER, complexity, and depth of images, Elliott Eisner (2002) stated that "many of the most complex and subtle forms of thinking take place when students have an opportunity either to work meaningfully on the creation of images . . . or to scrutinize them appreciatively"

(p. xi). Beyond meaning ten thousand words, as in the Chinese proverb, communicating through images contributes to the development of specific cognitive processes. Eisner (1991, 2002) has written extensively on how visual arts education contributes to developing cognitively demanding *somatic knowledge*, knowledge where an individual learns "how to use sight to inform feeling" (2002, pp. 75–76). This is a powerful and necessary tool as we seek to engage in educational processes that take into consideration the entire human being, the whole individual.

To be able to guide students in such forms of thinking, expanding their repertoire of cognitive processes, teachers in all subject areas (not only arts educators) need opportunities to activate their own imaginative capacities and practice the "ability to undergo emotionally pervaded experience" (Eisner, 2002, p. xii). The rational, language-based approach to most educational practices often leaves emotional and embodied ways of knowing untouched and unpracticed. Thus, in many ways, as educators, we talk the talk, but don't walk the walk (hooks, 1994). In this chapter, we present a technique called Image Theatre. Image Theatre offers a way to begin identifying issues and representing the presence of multiple dimensions and complexities, such as emotions and positionalities in educational settings.

RELEASING THE IMAGINATION

The primary goal of Image Theatre is to leave language behind as a primary communication tool and to rehearse the visual and kinesthetic. By using Image Theatre with teachers, we hope to cultivate experiences that release them, if only temporarily, from depending on the fixed meanings of words, and to exercise the fluidity and multiplicity of the imagination. Image Theatre allows participants to see the cultural nature of knowledge and to consider multiple perspectives, such important processes in multicultural education. Image Theatre values firsthand knowledge and builds on the situated representations of phenomena and their varying meanings to individual participants.

By sharing the ways in which we have employed Image Theatre in education, we hope to embrace multiple interpretations and perspectives as well as the emotional aspects of situations that are often left unspoken. We seek to break away from scripted curricula and standardized practices, as we illustrate how the very same image transacts with each individual in very particular ways, resulting in a gamut of meanings.

As with Games (Chapter 3), Image Theatre continues to promote a feeling of play connected to our first empirical experiences of the world.

Children start reading the world and mirroring its social practices at a very young age. Young children mime picking up the phone, stirring a pot, hunting like a tiger—freedom, creativity, and imagination are what make it possible for children to extend known experiences to the unknown, seeing and experiencing their own world and "creating what lies beyond it" (Eisner, 2002 p. 4). Such behaviors mirrored in children's play serve specific purposes and enact particular social practices. By mirroring observed actions through play, children start identifying and performing behaviors. As children grow to become adults, they are often reminded to live in the "real world," accepting what is and adapting to existing norms and structures. As adults, those who do not accommodate accordingly often become labeled as deviants or delinquents. Practices that primordially value the similarities among individuals while nipping differences in the bud make such spaces for creativity and imagination rare.

To imagine spaces for possibilities and change, teachers must constantly negotiate what "is" with what "could be," navigating within and across existing structures (e.g., from attendance taking to test administration to curriculum guidelines). Nevertheless, while trying to find wiggle room within such structures, it is also important to challenge and change those structures, especially when teachers perceive them to inhibit students' progress or unfairly advantage some students over others. Paulo Freire (1970) posited that the first step toward change and transformation is becoming aware of an issue. Image Theatre allows individuals to become personally and collectively aware of issues that affect their lives, so that they can move toward promoting change. When employed in teacher education, we have found that Image Theatre serves as an invitation for participants to move away from strictly using words to describe a fixed reality toward using visual and kinesthetic modalities, becoming aware of issues that are often lost in verbal retellings. Thus, Image Theatre allows teachers to move away from how to behave in the "real world" as teachers. Even scripted curriculum guides typically detail word-for-word what a teacher should say, but not necessarily how a teacher's body is to be positioned. The focus is on words. By engaging in wordless spaces for identification of issues, Image Theatre has the potential to work as a tool for creativity, imagination, freedom, and change even within constricted spaces such as scripted curricula.

Boal's Image Theatre requires participants to become human sculptors and sculptees—participants are simultaneously the force making the decision and the material to be molded. Working in small groups, participants collectively identify issues or concerns affecting their lives. However, instead of discussing these, each participant uses fellow participants' bodies as clay and sculpts from their bodies a series of images that represent these issues/concerns/oppressions. Ultimately, the making of images—which may be literal or abstract—often gives great clarity to a situation and can provoke considerable questioning and debate as to how a problem might actually be tackled.

The following six image exercises invite teachers to portray what they see, picture what they feel, complicate relationships, illuminate the partiality of any one perspective, and rehearse heightened, physical kinds of attention to themselves and others. The same ground rules apply as those explained in Chapter 3 for Games.

THE IMAGE EXERCISES

COMPLETE THE IMAGE

Number of people: 10–16 (even numbers desirable)
Time: 10–20 minutes

Short Description and Goals: This is an effective introduction to image work. This activity encourages participants to be in "visual dialogue" (Boal, 1992, p. 120) with one another's human sculptures, then translate and extend those images to match their own lived experience. This image work heightens attention to the multiplicity of perspectives and interpretations that may exist in a single event—how might "the same" homework assignment or classroom instruction be seen differently by a teacher, administrator, parent, or student?

Joker's Rules

1. Ask a pair of spect-actors to shake hands and freeze.
2. Ask the remaining spect-actors about possible interpretations for the image before them:

   • What are their characters (father-son? principal-parent? business partners? two walls of a building)?
   • What situation are they in (reunion; trade agreement; baseball practice; World Trade Center on September 11, 2001)?

3. Ask others to shout out what could be going on—not "the answer," but a variety of answers that might be in the form of a museum title or a piece of character dialogue, exploring "real" and "supernatural" possibilities.

Example

While viewing two people shaking hands, participants called out a variety of titles and/or segments of dialogue (indicated by quotes):

JOKER: What do you see and hear from this image?
BETH: "Who are *you*?"
CARMEN: They've seen each other's faces, but they don't remember each other's names.
BARB: Suspicion.
MARSHA: "Do I have something stuck in my teeth?"
JOKER: What kind of situation could they be in?
BETH: "You killed my mom."
LIZA: He's saying to a dog, "Shake, good girl!"
CHARLES: They're a principal and a teacher.
DEBORA: She could be a new teacher coming to school.
JOKER: If it was a job interview, what do you think the result would be?
DEBORA: "Hired!"
JOKER: Why?
DEBORA: Because she's happy and smiling.

4. Tap one partner on the shoulder and ask him/her to sit down.
5. Ask spectators for wild and varied interpretations of the remaining half-image.

- Is this a lamppost?
- A dog giving a paw to its owner?
- A wealthy gentleman hailing a cab?

6. Then ask another volunteer to complete the image and change its meaning by placing him- or herself in a different, complementary position (see Figure 4.1).

Example

Joker taps one participant and asks him/her to sit down. Others interpret the remaining single-person image before them. Participants respond to the image and how the image becomes transformed:

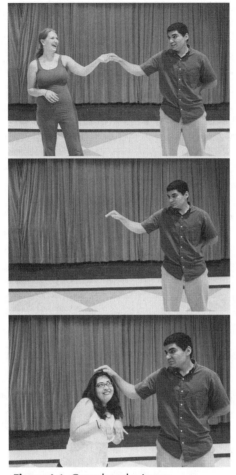

Figure 4.1. Complete the Image

LENA: She's reaching for something in the refrigerator.
RACHEL: "Guilt at the Refrigerator!"
RANDALL: She's thinking "Oh God, I think it's broken."
BARB: She's taking somebody's hand for a dance move.
STEVEN: "Help!"
MARSHA: This is the top part of a light, a street lamp.
STEVEN: She's trying to catch a cat.
JOKER: Trying to catch a cat. Good! Now hold on there for a

second; somebody else come add yourself to this picture in
a different relationship, *not* shaking hands.
(*Marsha steps up and puts herself in front of Sara's extended hand
and puts her arms up in the air.*)
JOKER: (*group laughter*) What's going on here?
IAN: She's hitting her.
BETH: Or shooting her.
BARB: Holding her up, like robbing her.
BARB (*in a pitiful voice*): "Please stay, I *love* you!"
JOKER: And what's she saying?
BARB: "I can't take it anymore!"
JOKER: What else, a different story.
PATTON: "No, I won't make spaghetti again!"
(*Big group laugh.*)
JOKER: Thank you, relax, let's give everybody a round of
    applause.
(*Everyone claps for the pairs.*)

Depending on time, the Joker can continue to tap one individual and invite others to enter the half-sculpture and change
its meaning.

Variation

1. All players form pairs and continue this exercise independently
   around the room—forming a complementary image and then taking turns leaving the image, observing it, and changing the meaning by adding a new, complementary half-image. This should be
   done without conversation and in silence.
2. Encourage literal or imaginary meaning-making; ask participants
   to enter a dreamlike state and to keep their half- and full images
   moving. Here, it is important for partners to maintain a sense of
   flow and exchange.
3. Take 5 to 10 minutes to experience this exercise.

Extension

1. Ask pairs to incorporate an object or objects into their moving
   images (e.g., a chair, lamp, bookbag, table).
2. Encourage teams to discuss answers to these questions:

   • How does the object change the dynamic (Boal, 1992)?

- Does choice of object (or mandate of a certain object to be incorporated) influence the dynamic?

Discussion: Have a large-group discussion, considering the following questions:

- How did you feel?
- Was the exercise fun? Difficult?
- Notice your impulses: Did you tend to dominate the exercise? Did you follow the other person's lead?
- How might this exercise serve as a metaphor for teaching and learning?

Participants' Reflections: In the dialogue below, participants reflect on how this activity illuminates teaching as a responsive activity.

VANESSA: In this game, you never know what the other person is going to do, and then once they do it, you try to feed off of that. I noticed that I wanted to do something that was pleasing to the other person, not just anything. You want to complement what the other person is doing.

PETER: I just liked the surprise that would come, you know? Often, we would be creating relationship shapes where one person couldn't see the other, and so you had to sense when the other person was there and then you would come out of it and almost see the ghost image of what was and then go "Oh, yeah, okay." There was that element of surprise in it.

TERESITA: I also felt like we were communicating without language.

JORGE: So connecting it to teaching, it's give and take; it's a dialogue. This game and teaching, they're both like a dance. You do one thing, the other person responds, and you respond to that. It's a give-and-take situation.

ELIZABETH: That's how teaching is, really. It's a give-and-take. It's not all teacher-centered or all student-centered. It's both.

MARCIA: What's interesting is, when you make a movement, you have an expectation of how the other person's going to respond. If they don't respond that way, you wonder: Did I miscommunicate using my body language or did they just have a different interpretation?

AMANDA: It's like problem solving with creativity!

MEGHAN: Yeah, like when you're a student teacher you have to walk a fine line between follower and leader. You have to be creative because sometimes you have to follow what your cooperating teacher says and other times you have to take the bull by the horns!

Participants were clearly able to articulate how this activity related to teaching. This activity allowed them to collectively imagine and blur the roles of leader and follower, of actor and spectator, of teacher and learner. According to their reflections, this activity signified the complexity and blurring of such dynamic and ever-changing roles.

COME, MY FRIENDS . . .

Number of people: Any number
Time: 5–20 minutes

Short Description and Goals: Often, the first way we recognize one another is through what M. Weinblatt (personal communication, May 29, 2005) called "the body suit," the physical package of our body that displays (mis)information about our identities in terms of age, race, gender, ability, and so forth. Appearances can often hide important details of experience. For example, our first impression in many courses for pre-service early childhood educators is that many of our students were homogeneous-looking. Many appeared to be similarly young, female, and White. However, even in the most homogenous-looking groups, there are both commonalities and differences that appear when more information is known about each individual. Using Image Theatre to examine categories of belonging provides an excellent opportunity for individuals to discover common experiences as well as different perspectives within what seems to be the same group. Although we all have universal needs (e.g., to sleep, to eat, to love, to grieve), some of our cultural practices may differ (or not). Recognizing the complexities of sameness within difference and difference within sameness is a major contribution of this activity.

Joker's Rules

1. Ask participants to think of categories in which they belong, imagining wild and varied types of categories (e.g., first-year teachers, mango lovers, garage sale specialists, etc.).
2. Form a large circle and ask participants, one by one, to come to the middle of the circle and call out a category, saying, "Come, my friends who are . . ." One rule is that it is everyone's right to identify or not identify with a category, and no one can volunteer or

force another person into an identity (e.g., no nudging someone saying, "Go! Go! You are a ping pong player!"). If, for any reason, a participant does not wish to identify with a category, she or he does not need to enter the circle. Remember, "friends" may form a category of one or may include the entire group—it all depends.

3. Once the friends are gathered in the center, call out, "Family image!" The group has about 5 seconds, without talking, to sculpt themselves into an image that conveys what, according to their perspectives, it feels like to belong to this group (see Figure 4.2).

Participants' Responses: Teachers began with professional identities and jumped to more personal and social identities through the course of the exercise.

> JORGE: How about if I say, "Come, my friends who are high school teachers"?
>
> JOKER: High school teachers, all high school teachers come to the middle.
>
> (*Jorge and others enter the circle.*)
>
> JOKER: Form a "family image" by sculpting your bodies in a way that tells us how it feels to be a high school teacher. (*One*

Figure 4.2. Come, My Friends . . .

teacher arches her body backwards and throws her arms toward the
ceiling. Another tangles her arms in a knot and then pulls them to her
forehead. The spectators in the circle start laughing.) Awesome!
(*sighs*) Freeze. We got it! (*to those observing*). Do we feel it? Do
we feel it? Thank you! You may return.

DORI: How about, "Come, my friends who are newly certified"?

JOKER: Newly certified. Anyone who has just gotten certification
(*walking and pointing toward the middle of the circle*). What does
that feel like? Family image!

(*Five teachers enter the circle. One is looking outward with her hands*
clasped to her cheeks. Another has her head tilted slightly downward and
her palms lifted up to the sky. Another has her head thrown back dramati-
cally with the back of her hand brushing her brow. Another is slumped
over with her hands on her knees. They convey a sense of exhaustion or
relief.)

JOKER: (*laughing*) Can we relate? (*The group drops the pose and heads*
back to the circle. Many say yes.) Thank you.

JODY: How about provisional certification? "Come, my friends who
have provisional certification."

(*Joker gestures toward the center of the circle and participants anticipate*
the call for a "family image." Jody runs in, makes a small high-pitched
noise and draws her forearms toward her chest with her fingers extended
like a dead bug. Another teacher is on her knees, with her face tilted to the
ceiling and her hands thrown up. The circle laughs and the group returns
to their seats.)

ALYSSA: What about working and going to school? Do I have any
friends? (*murmurs of "Yes" around the circle.*) Yeah. (*Alyssa is*
doubled over with her hands clasped behind her neck. Other people
are pulling their hair and clutching their foreheads. One teacher is
pretending that she is pounding with her fists on Alyssa's back.)

YOLANDA: Um, I'll call one. "*Vengan mis amigos*! If you're the only
Latino teacher in your school." (*Several people start walking.*)

JOKER: Family image! (*The group in the center is making their pose*
amid giggles from the group. There are six. Yolanda is in a boxing
stance, looking ready for a fight.)

Variations

- Ask participants to form a single, unified image. For example, rather
  than separate interpretations of what it means to "work and go to
  school," the group would have time to discuss and present a single
  image from the collective group of bodies. Hence, three individuals

might pose together in an active triptych (like the famous image portrayed for the American 1970s sitcom *Charlie's Angels*, but with car keys, books, and children in their hands rather than weapons).

• A large group may remain seated around the room and simply rise from their chairs to illustrate their belonging to the group, creating their pose from wherever they may be located.

COLUMBIAN HYPNOSIS

Number of people: 6–18 (depending on room size; even numbers desirable)
Time: 15–20 minutes

Short Description and Goals: A variation on "follow the leader," this activity helps participants cultivate both a physical and social awareness of others. Through leader/follower role-play, the idiom "Lead as you would like to be led" becomes vivified, and players raise questions about power in teachers' relationships with others, including students, parents, administrators, district leaders, and politicians. Because of the length of this exercise, it's easy to notice how stressful it can be to follow the leader, whoever that leader may be, over time. Although it is okay to pretend to play along for a short period of time, it can become very stressful over more extended periods of time. This activity can be physically demanding, so it is best to encourage partners to wear comfortable clothing, removing shoes if possible, and playing with a small number of pairs who can comfortably move about the room.

Joker's Rules

1. Demonstrate this process in the front of the room, inviting a pair of participants to step forward, one of whom will "hypnotize" the other. Partner A (the hypnotist) puts his or her open hand 6 to 8 inches from Partner B's face, fingertips in line with the forehead, palm in line with the chin. Partner B becomes mesmerized by Partner A's hand, which guides Partner B to move in new and unexpected ways. Partner B is to follow Partner A in real time (see Figure 4.3).
2. After the demonstrations, have all participants work in pairs.
3. Have the Partner As lead for approximately 3 to 5 minutes. As participants are engaged in the activity, ask the Partner As to notice how it feels to lead and the Partner Bs to notice how it feels to follow.
4. Tell the Partner As to "release the spell."

Figure 4.3. Columbian Hypnosis

5. Tell the partners to switch roles. Ask partners to notice the differences between leading and following.
6. After both partners have had a chance to lead, instruct both partners to lead *and* follow at the same time, each placing a hand in front of the other's face, guided by his or her own rhythms and instincts.
7. Encourage pairs to experiment, modifying participation so they enjoy it better or experience a new dimension of the play.

Cautions: This is a nonverbal exercise, so any movements that the following partner cannot complete must be expressed physically. Slow movements and transitions are recommended to prevent dizziness or exasperation. Remind participants of the ethics of reciprocity, as partners will soon exchange roles!

Extensions

- Ask participants to form groups of three, four, or more, leading and following the whole group (complaints will arise, but it can be done!).
- Instruct participants to lead and follow in a manner different from what they did before—in compassionate ways; in oppressive, domi-

neering ways; in rebellious ways; and so on. What happens when you follow like a sheepdog versus following like the Tasmanian devil? How might followers control their leaders? How can each partner bring more humor or more seriousness to his or her team?

- Encourage teams to discuss answers to these questions and then have a large-group discussion:

    How did it feel to lead? To follow?
    How different did it feel to lead and follow at the same time?
    Did you tend to play one role more than the other?
    Did you prefer one role over another?
    In what ways does this exercise evoke issues related to status and
        power?

Participants' Reflections on the Exercise: In this dialogue, participants reflected on the impact their social roles (e.g., race, gender, and so forth) and cultural practices had on how they engaged in the activity.

TERI: I was struck by how responsible I felt when I was the hypnotizer, that I was trying to read her body and I wanted to challenge her but I didn't want to make her uncomfortable. I wanted a sense of caring and responsibility. There was a little anxiety but because she responded positively, I guess it was okay.

STEVEN: I didn't like to follow. I just didn't like the fact that I had to follow [Beth's] . . . hand, and I didn't want to go to the floor at all, and [Beth] . . . said she could sense my resistance, but she took me down there anyway! She's like my exact opposite, and I felt out of control.

BETH: Can I throw something out there? I was telling Steven that when I moved my hand down, I knew he didn't want to because he was staying on his feet and I was like, well, because I'm a White woman and he's a Black man, I didn't want to make him go all the way down and then I thought that's kind of the point, right? So I did.

JOKER: It doesn't really matter how you play. What's important is what you notice in the experience and what histories become a part of the story you are now playing, both individually and socially, without words.

LIZA: I think in our pair [with Rosa], we both felt very comfortable when we were following each other and directing at the same time.

Rosa: I was just thinking that because we're close to the same age and kind of similar, I felt more comfortable playing with her a little bit because I could read her expression and read her body really well. When she got tense, I'd stop what I was doing. With somebody else, I might not push it as much—not that I pushed her a whole lot, but I did back her across the room! (*laughs*)

Joker: How many of you liked the simultaneous relationship as opposed to the other one where there was a clear leader/ follower?

Beth: I was just surprised when I had to follow because in real life I am *not* a follower. I'm always amazed at how easily people will follow others without thinking about it. After this game, I feel I understand that better because, as a follower, I didn't really have to *do* anything. I had no responsibility and it was really easy just to do what my partner told me to do, you know?

Joker [to Steven, Beth's partner]: Did you have fun leading her around?

Steven: No, I didn't really like it. I felt like I was getting her and then I asked myself why I was making her do something and she's just doing it for no reason. I didn't like it.

Participants' Reflections on Teaching: In this dialogue, participants reflected on the ways working simultaneously as leader and follower resonated with what it means to be a teacher.

Jorge: When we were leading and following together, it felt like a dance. I had to be careful, where she was leading me and also where she was going. So it really felt like we were doing the tango. We had to have a certain distance and still be assertive.

Clarissa: I felt most comfortable when I was both the hypnotizer and the hypnotizee because I didn't feel I was totally responsible. I felt I was being fair because I was working *with* someone else, not just telling that person what to do. And I was getting feedback.

Rosa: I really liked doing it together; it was like cooperating. While I was leading I was thinking, "Where am I leading her?" When we did it both together, we were thinking, "Where are we leading *each other*?" I think in education it's the same thing. You know, "Where am I leading the students? And are they cooperating, are we walking together toward the same goals?"

AMANDA: For me, it was really interesting the way we established another way to communicate. It's not only by words, but it's in the look in her eyes. I think it's good for the educators because you learn to read your audience. Students don't need to say, "I don't understand what you're talking about it" or "What is going on?" because as a teacher I can see it in their faces or in their bodies. This game simulated that ability to read another person, to know when you have to slow down. It felt really good to practice that.

RACHEL: I was also thinking about it from the perspective of working on a team of teachers at school and how difficult it must be to be the team leader. My team leader is a peer of mine, and we have about the same level of experience. It must be so difficult for her to feel like she has to know where she's leading us. Next year the role reverses, and I'll be in that position, and I need to think about what it means for me to be a colleague leading other peer colleagues.

VANESSA: Just piggy-backing on what Rachel was saying, this is also true in terms of the administration. One of the assistant principals at my school is probably younger than my oldest son. So to take orders from him is a bit tricky. His age and his role are things I really have to overcome so I can respect him. How much is he willing to let me lead? How much am I willing to respect his leadership?

Participating teachers could clearly articulate the value of this activity in understanding the complexities involved in interpersonal relationships involving administrators, students, or colleagues. They could also associate this activity with the many issues involved in communicating across and within cultural groups.

THE MACHINE: BUILDING INTERRELATIONS

Number of people: 8–20
Time: 5–10 minutes

Short Description and Goals: This activity illustrates the larger structures within which individuals are part. As participants work together, they seek to create a whole that is more meaningful than the sum of its parts. Because of this interdependence, for this activity to work well each person has to listen carefully to everything she or he hears, responding to it accordingly. It also illustrates the potential of transformation, even if change starts small. As one piece of the machine changes, others will, too, or the machine will not work as intended. According to Boal (1992), it's "extraordinary how the ideology of a group, its political standpoint, can be revealed in a rhythm of sound and movement. The way people think and the things they find fault with soon become apparent" (p. 91).

Joker's Rules

1. Begin with a title for the machine. For example, announce:

   Today we are going to build the "Education Machine." Everyone will think of all the components that make up this machine. I will invite you one by one to come into the center of the room and create the parts of the machine. You are encouraged to interact/respond to other parts until we have a cacophony of sound and movements that compose this working thing we call "Education."

2. Have the first actor enter the machine and perform his or her sound and movement.
3. Ask that "piece" to be silent while a second "piece" is added by another actor.
4. Instruct each piece to produce sounds and movements and then be silent to welcome each new piece until all members of the troupe are a part of one machine.
5. Ask the troupe to simultaneously begin making their noise and movement quietly (see Figure 4.4).
6. As a conductor, raise your hands and arms upward, asking the group to increase their noise level and pacing until the machine takes on a frenetic quality.
7. Raise and lower the level of the machine noise/movement.
8. Tap individuals to turn them "off" (one tap) or "on" (two taps).

Extensions

- When the machine is ready, ask if the first person wants to accelerate the rhythm. Everyone else adjusts to this new and accelerated rhythm. "When the machine is near to explosion, the Joker asks the first person to ease up, gradually to slow down, till in their own time the whole group ends together" (Boal, 1992, p. 90).
- Ask the machine to turn off and on several times, at varying intervals.

Figure 4.4. The Machine

- Ask the machine to accelerate or decelerate according to the task called out—e.g., parent-teacher conferences (accelerate), winter holidays (decelerate).

Variations

- Start with one person making a moving part of a machine and others joining in as complementary parts of the machine. Then ask those observing and those participating what the machine is.
- Create two (or more) machines that serve the same purpose. Follow up with dialogue about the functions and forms undertaken by each machine.

Participants' Reflections: Following this activity, participants expressed their understanding of how, even in their own classroom, all pieces have to work together (students and teachers), but also that there are machines within machines—their classroom, the school, the school district, the state Department of Education, and the U.S. Department of Education. While they all must work together, change can start small and can be initiated by an individual or by a small group. They also expressed their renewed belief in listening to all the pieces of the machine so that it can work more efficiently and with fewer unnecessary stressors.

IMAGE TECHNIQUES: THE MODEL

Number of people: 10–40
Time: 20–35 minutes

Short Description and Goals: This activity engages participants in multiple phases of constructing a model. Some or all may be employed, depending on the time available and the level of interest. A volunteer uses the bodies of other participants to sculpt an image, a model that represents a certain phenomenon, subject, or concept. This is a process of constructing something while negotiating with a group that is providing guidelines, evaluation, and some assistance, but not engaging in active co-construction. After completion, if participants approve the image representing a certain phenomenon, the model is kept; otherwise, it is rejected, and as a result, it is taken apart and the activity begins anew. If the group approves the model with reservations (suggesting a revision and resubmission of the model), the builder/sculptor consults the group as he seeks to revise the model until it is satisfactory according to functionality and meaning.

Joker's Rules

Make it clear there are many phases to this image activity. (These are divided into several parts below.)

Part I. Creating an Image

1. Ask participants to stand facing outward in a circle, imagining how they would sculpt their bodies to express a selected role in a visual form (e.g., "the teacher" or "the student" or "Superman").
2. Ask all participants, when they hear a handclap, to turn inward and take on a formal pose that represents this role (e.g., all become their own visions of "the teacher"). All images should be static, even if they are caught mid-movement (e.g., a teacher writing on a chalkboard; a teacher lecturing a class; a teacher working in a small group, and so on).
3. Ask all participants to maintain their frozen position and scan other images of "the teacher" around the circle. As a variation (Creating Missing Images), ask participants to scan the circle and call out "Addition!" if they can suggest an image different from those that are already shown.

Part II. Connecting to Other Images

4. Once all images have been formed, ask participants to listen for a handclap and move toward what they feel are kindred images, thereby forming a family image. This should be done without speaking and only through visual recognition. Participants should try to move, to the extent possible, while maintaining their image.
5. Ask each "family" to freeze together in their collective image, and then clap to release each family. Silently, participants walk around and notice the similarities and differences between individuals in the family.

Part III. Responding to Images

6. Ask one family to re-form their images, and ask each individual member to think of a title for that family.
7. Have each participant share his or her title while maintaining a static pose. Do the titles convey a sense of relationship between the images?

Part IV. Completing the Image

8. Ask each individual in the selected family to "complete the image," moving to the next logical pose to follow the first (e.g., a teacher with a hand to the chalkboard might move his/her hand downward). With a second handclap, each returns to the first image, then the second; the first, then the second.
9. Ask the observing actors to propose titles for the family of moving images.

Part V. Images That Speak

10. Ask all family participants to simultaneously add one sentence to their dynamized pair of movements.
11. Then ask only one person at a time to share their sentence/movements (see Figure 4.5).
12. Repeat this with all families or as many as time permits.

Example

CARMIN: (*holding arms in front of her as if carrying a large rock, then lifting the weight over her head*) The weight of the world, the weight of the world.

Figure 4.5. The Weight of the World

JOKER: Next.

MANKA: (*hands in front of her in running position, then raising hands and jumping*) Yippieee! (*repeating movement*) Yippieee.

LIZA: (*like Carmin, holding arms in front of her as if carrying a large rock, then lifting the weight over her head*) The world is in my hands, the world is in my hands.

CARA: (*like Carmin and Liza, holding arms in front of her as if carrying a large rock, then moving forward and embracing hands and arms around an object*). Good job! (*repeating the "hug"*) Good job!

JOKER: Okay, thanks. (*applause*) Okay, so in each family, there was a lot of different opinions of what the teacher was, no? Let's move to another family. The family that was here.

(*The next group moves to their corner and the process is repeated*).

Part VI. Transitioning the Image (an Extension)

13. Return to Part I and ask participants to sculpt themselves in an opposite or complementary image (e.g., if the first was "teacher," the second may be "student"; see Figure 4.6).

Figure 4.6. Image Techniques: The Many Faces of "The Student"

14. Call out the first and the second roles, and ask participants to slowly move between them.
15. Have the actors discuss what they observe and relate it to their experiences with each role.

Example

Joker calls out, "teacher," then "student," asking the group to scan the circle to observe their peer-actors

JOKER: What is the difference between them?
CARMIN: The teacher poses are frustrated when the students are not.
RANDALL: Not all of them; for some, the students are more frustrated than the teachers.
MANKA: The students have more closed postures than the teachers.
LIZA: It seems like the teachers are more in control.
CARA: Well, some of us look more positive as the teacher and some of us look more positive as the student. The teachers and students have different agendas.

JOKER: Do you think teachers are aware of these different agendas?

LIZA: I think we all have good intentions to get to know our students, but I don't think that consistently happens. Either because of lack of time or lack of willingness—even on the students' parts! Sometimes you try to make an attempt to get to know them and then they shut down. So how do you connect? You know, it's a process; it's not just goodwill.

YOLANDA: It depends on the level that you teach. Because I teach high school now and there's no way one of them gets to know me. They don't want me to get to know them better, and I have over 100 students a day.

ALISSA: But I think it's not really good to expect teachers to be parents. I mean I feel a lot of responsibility toward my students, but I also want to go home and have my own relationships with my friends and my partner, and when I can't do that, I'm not a very nice person. You know? (*laughter*) So I feel like all my life is taken away from me because I signed a contract and I didn't sign up to be a parent. I signed up to be a teacher.

YOLANDA: And some parents are expecting us to raise their child.

DORI: But don't you think maybe the right information is not given to the parents, so they don't know what is expected of them? For example, parents from Latin American countries often believe showing respect for the teacher is to leave everything up to them because they're the experts. So they have a misperception of what the parent's role should be.

YOLANDA: I think you're misconstruing what I'm saying. I'm saying that I'm not going to become that child's counselor, social worker, you know, whatever.

ALISSA: Sometimes the teachers are the only help the students and parents have.

LIZA: This relates to our family of images! Last year was my first year of teaching and I used to come home feeling like I was carrying the burdens of the world. And one of the teachers, I won't forget this, she said, "You know, you can't save them all." And I finally realized that I can't save them all. But I can extend my kindness. I think as teachers we have a moral obligation to genuinely care about them and their well-being. And that's all we can do. I mean I can't control what goes on beyond my classroom. But while they're in there in that classroom for 90 minutes, if I can make them feel safe, if I can make them feel respected, if I can make them feel like, you know, they *want* to be there, then I feel like, you know what? I succeeded. You know, it was a good day. That's all you can do.

REAL/IDEAL

Number of people: 5–25
Time: 5–20 minutes

Short Description and Goals: According to Augusto Boal (1992), the real/ideal activity signified "the beginnings of Image Theatre" (p. 2). Building on Part I of the previous exercise, Real/Ideal works by generating a visual argument without words. This visual argument is able to access both micro- and macro-level aspects of oppression. The goal is to bring forth revealing and unexpected aspects of a social role or concept and to raise individual and collective options for change.

Joker's Rules

1. Ask spectactors to form groups and work on a *real* image of oppression related to a specific theme (e.g., teachers as oppressed professionals; public education as an oppressed social institution).
2. Ask individuals in the group to each construct an *ideal* image of the same theme in which the oppression no longer exists for the whole or its parts (individuals may work separately or as a unit).
3. Ask the group to form their real image and then their ideal image several times (real/ideal dyads may be performed individually or as a unit).
4. Ask each actor to slowly model and/or sculpt what changes each would have to make in order to transition between the real and ideal postures without words. Notice the small movements and changes between the two poles.
5. Study all possibilities for liberation and their phases of transition, and ask participants for a "reality check" (further described in Chapter 5):

   • How real is the proposed transition and "ideal" image?
   • Will there be a movement and posture that resolves the oppression?

Variations

- Ask a group of individuals to form a collective image of "real" op-pression. Ask one individual outside the group to sculpt each ele-ment of the "real" into the "ideal." Discuss the proposed solutions—do they represent real possibilities or magic?
- Ask each participant to speak when they are in the "real" image and again when they are in the "ideal" image. How do their shapes determine what is said and how it is said in each position? Ask one "real" and one "ideal" image to be in dialogue with one another.
- Choose concepts or roles that may have two sides of an oppressive circumstance (e.g., the oppression of "the teacher" and the oppres-sion of "the student" or "the administrator"; "male" and "female" experiences). This can be especially powerful when working with mixed groups and enables each group to see and/or generate the perspectives of the other. Might each group embody aspects of the oppressed and the oppressor?

Participants' Responses: When asked to create a "real" image of a category of privilege that made them feel uncomfortable (see "Power Shuffle" game in Chapter 3), one group chose social class and described themselves as growing up having "More Than Enough" relative to peers. Participants in this group titled their first "real" image "Hunger" and described the dis-comfort associated with class privilege.

> The "Hunger" statue involved three females who were kneeling and eating out of a garbage can, while two others stood, facing the garbage can. All other participants walked slowly around the image and called out titles and/or segments of dialogue.

> JOKER: As we walk around, those on the outside of the group will say one word or phrase that comes to mind while observing this image.
> CRISTINA: Poverty.
> MARSHA: Trash.
> JOSÉ: Solitude.
> CARMELITA: Compassion.
> CARMEN: Charity.
> CRISTINA: Sorrow.
> MADALENA: Hardship.

JORGE: Necessity.

JOKER: If you would, speak in the voices of these various characters and say what it is that they're thinking.

MARSHA: Should I give? I guess I should give to *these* people.

JOKER: Someone from the image, tell us what is going on for you.

CATHERINE: What we did when we were growing up was we *gave*, but I always felt we should have done more. I've always been hungry to know how they felt, the poor. How I could help? I was always sorry as a child to have what I had and that other people didn't.

ANA: Well, I mean, for me this was difficult. I grew up in Brazil, and I remember the first time I realized how unequal things were was when I was like 6 or 7 years old, and I saw a child my own age eating out of a trash can, and I just asked myself: Number one, why does that child have to do it? and number two, why can I go home and have a nice meal? And just at that moment, I started questioning and it's something I've never gotten over. I always have that child's face in my head.

After this discussion, the group proceeded to create the ideal from the real. Together, they transformed that real image into an ideal action or image. The ideals are not always concrete ideas and images, but may involve a concept such as collectivity or togetherness. This group created an image of collective engagement and commitment, signified by a blossom made of human bodies (see Figure 4.7). They embraced the issue, rather than ignoring it, and became unified, blossoming together.

IMAGING THE WORLD, IMAGINING THE POSSIBILITIES

Overall, the aim of creating an image is compatible with Freire's (1970) idea of identifying and naming issues in order to problematize and change them. Making commonplace issues visible and thinking about transforming them is one of the many contributions afforded by such image work. Image Theatre techniques have the power to disrupt the commonplace by making differences visible, problematizing subjects of study, and understanding existing knowledge as sociocultural and historical products (Shor, 1987). Furthermore, it provides openings in which participants can start interrogating multiple viewpoints, making difference visible and examining competing narratives and writing counternarratives to dominant discourses (Harste, Lewison, Leland, Ociepka, & Vasquez, 2000).

Figure 4.7. Real/Image: Blossom

The image exercises presented in this chapter provide learning cases and examples from our work with teachers. We invite you to envision ways in which these images can become part of your setting as you seek to name, problematize, and transform issues. We hope you will imagine the image and invite colleagues and students to join you, starting the process of collectively imaging the world and imagining change.

Forum Theatre: Telling Stories of Teacher Conflict and Rehearsing Change

A TEACHER's daily life is filled with stories—funny anecdotes, frustrating roadblocks, sad reckonings, joyful surprises. Teachers work in classrooms, frequently isolated from colleagues and professors, but assemble in work-rooms, cafeterias, parking lots, or university corridors to share their stories and to connect with one another. These spaces provide opportunities for problem solving via storytelling (Allen & Hermann-Wilmarth, 2004; Ochs, Smith, & Taylor, 1996). Such forums often happen at the margins of official, professional spaces. They may occur frequently or sporadically. Often, whether or not teachers can count on each other to problem solve is left to chance, to the possibility that they might see each other in the

Portions of this chapter are reprinted or adapted from two earlier journal articles; we thank the Journal of Early Childhood Teacher Education and Teachers College Record for allowing us to use them here.

workroom, for example. But what happens when teachers face problems that are concrete, recurring, and urgent? When and where are there forums for teachers to revisit professional challenges with students, colleagues, parents, professors, and others, and to rehearse new alternatives?

As teachers and education professors, we are very practiced at advice-giving: Oh, you have trouble with a student who won't sit in his seat? Have you tried asking him to help you teach a lesson? Have you tried separating his seat from the group? Why don't you do this? I would do that! Advisors are everywhere, and they may frequently shape the way a teacher may view her or his role (Rymes, 1996). But advice can be a form of what Boal (1992) referred to as "evangelism," whereby the advisor's words, especially when given from a place of authority, are meant to be taken as the absolute answer to an advisee's problems and the path toward their salvation. A critical stance toward pedagogy, however, seeks more Socratic methods, believing the answers to our problems are often multiple, contextual, and dialogic. Such a stance acknowledges that authority is fluid and dialectically negotiated (Foucault, 1978; Kincheloe, 2005). Furthermore, a critical stance toward pedagogy recognizes the importance of situated knowledges and contextual framings (Souto-Manning, 2010).

Building upon warm-up games and images, we used "Forum Theatre" as a means to place privately experienced, recurring struggles in classrooms and schools as the central focus in pre-service and in-service teacher education. This approach moves away from canned, ready solutions to problems, solutions that ignore the interactional and contextual complexities of classrooms, schools, and society.

FORUM THEATRE: FOUNDATIONS FOR CREATING CHANGE

In our minds, Forum Theatre is the central structure that drives most of the other Theatre of the Oppressed activities. The Games (Chapter 3) and Image Exercises (Chapter 4) warm up our participants for Forum Theatre, in which teachers can tackle their day-to-day interpersonal struggles and begin to see the interconnectedness between their own challenges and those experienced by others in the world at large. Forum Theatre provides fertile grounds for addressing the questions: What does one teacher's conflict reveal about the educational profession at large, and how might this conflict relate to larger social, cultural, and economic issues?

Boal (1992) asserted that the central intention of Forum Theatre is to "transform the spectator into the Protagonist of the theatrical action and, by this transformation, to try to change society rather than contenting ourselves with interpreting it" (p. 4). Our goals in advocating the use of Forum Theatre in teachers' professional training is to help increase the numbers of educators who see themselves as truly capable of promoting change. We intend to cultivate a learning environment in which participants rehearse living in multiplicity, creating alternative realities, and expanding opportunities for action. We aim to move away from simplistic answers to issues that are made complex by situated contexts and multiple interactions. Further, we want to move away from the knowledge-as-truth paradigm as we seek to develop culturally responsive and situated perspectives that honor and affirm diversities. Finally, we seek to reframe conflicts as opportunities for learning and for transforming, instead of something that must (at all costs) be avoided (Cahnmann, 2001).

Ideally, Forum Theatre is a process that is cultivated over several sessions of games and image work that warms the group up to share participants' most deeply felt struggles and to collectively rehearse these struggles for individual and group change. This allows a sense of trust to be developed through which a community of teachers who are also learners emerges. Through multiyear grants and semester-long courses during the 2003–2009 period, we often had experiences working with the same group over a period of weeks and years. However, we also introduced Forum Theatre during 3-hour workshops at professional conferences and by invitation to schools and school districts. At the American Council on the Teaching of Foreign Languages (ACTFL) annual convention, for example, during a 3-hour session, we were able to share a few warm-up games and move into Forum Theatre work concerning struggles with disinterested Spanish Level One students (Wooten & Cahnmann-Taylor, 2007). In contrast, we attended a 45-minute session that tried to tackle a case of racism, but there was not enough time for the group to really examine the multifaceted and sensitive nature of the situation.

We would like to propose the need to refuse and refute the concept of panoptical time (Foucault, 1977). According to Lesko (2001), "panoptical gaze produces control through normalization . . . linear, historical time moving toward 'progress' [must] be examined for how it disciplines subjectivities and objective knowledge" (p. 111). We want to avoid normalizing situations due to time constraints, as the very premise of this work is to explore possibilities, re-enact situations, and rehearse change through multiple renderings. Thus, we recommend a minimum time frame of 2 to 3 hours for a Forum Theatre workshop in order to deeply and powerfully engage with teachers' lived concerns in a way that dignifies complexity and deepens understanding.

HOW FORUM THEATRE WORKS: GENERATING SHARED DOUBTS AND CONCERNS

After warming up with a series of games and image work, we start each Forum Theatre session by having participants share their struggles and concerns—many of which may have already been alluded to in the warmup exercises. We ask pre- and in-service teachers to narrate recurring stories of conflict and position themselves as "protagonists" during interactions with "antagonist" others. The generative themes that emerge through stories of conflict represent diverse situations and include struggles with a range of "antagonists," including administrators, students, colleagues, paraprofessionals, parents, and college professors (see Figure 5.1).

Once stories are shared, the group collectively selects one story that represents a generative theme for the group. These stories may represent interpersonal conflicts with which all teachers can identify and/or those related to recurring social issues regarding race, class, or citizenship status and/or language proficiency. Boal (1992) emphasized the importance of "common interests" so individuals can relate personally to the conflict to be reenacted. Thus a democratic process is embraced whereby individuals share struggles and the collective votes on the story or stories that have the most resonance with the majority or entirety of the group. One-time-only grievances give way to recurring struggles that present the actual possibility of changing one's actions and transforming outcomes. Although

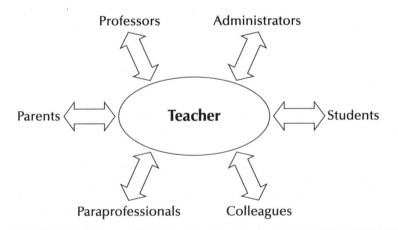

Figure 5.1. Generative Themes: Struggles Between a Teacher and Antagonists

the specifics of a case—e.g., the repeated bullying by a senior colleague in a math department who disparages a more junior faculty member's approach to algebra—may not be shared by each member in the group—the overall conflict, mistrust, and judgment concerning teaching expertise and hierarchies of status may be something that all teacher-participants can relate to.

Although the specific details of the generative case (e.g., a colleague acting in racist or unethical ways; a parent behaving belligerently; a professor who embodies the persona of an epistemological bully) are used to create a two- to three-scene drama, the selected story no longer belongs to the initiating storyteller but to the collective—whom Boal referred to as "spect-actors." As explained in Chapter 2, Boal (1979) coined the term *spect-actor* to break the divide between "spectator" and "actor." While the initial storyteller might first play the role of the protagonist, she or he is frequently replaced by other spect-actors in the group who identify with the protagonist and who perform alternative courses of action to change the outcome of the conflict. Thus rather than simply giving verbal advice to the storyteller, as typically occurs in the problem-solution, "banking approach" (Freire, 1970) of most teacher education contexts (e.g., "Why don't you try talking to your principal about this?"), spect-actors are encouraged to share the story by reliving it themselves. Spect-actors may get out of their seats, stepping into the protagonist's role and performing (e.g., becoming the teacher who schedules an appointment with the principal and role-playing themselves in the imagined dialogue). After each enactment, the Joker (the facilitator or "difficult-ator" of the session [Boal, 1979], as explained in Chapter 2) asks for a "reality check" to collectively determine the viability of the proposed strategy. This process is illustrated in cases presented later in this chapter.

As stated earlier (in Chapter 2), the goals of performing the texts of teachers' lived experiences are not to find absolute answers, but rather to seek options, to debate alternatives, and to cultivate a sense of multiplicity, flexibility, and possibilities for change. Spect-actors often accept or reject strategies based on whether they "feel right" or not (e.g., "I couldn't say/do that, I'd lose my job!"), which then leads to further enactment, strategizing, and reality checks in a recursive model of this performance-based focus group format. The end goal is not to convince others of one right model for behavior but rather to present an *anti-model* that "must always present doubt and not certainty" (Boal, 1992, p. 232). All parts of the anti-model are contested and recursive—deciding which stories we have to tell, and how to divide them up into rehearsable parts; choosing how to alter a scene, and deciding upon action. Forum Theatre rests upon doubt, improvisation, and dialogue.

The critical performative process (see Figure 5.2) includes five phases:

1. *What's the story?* The texts employed in the classroom are generated from the participants' lives, narratives, and experiences (Freire, 1970). These stories recount situations in which participants experienced recurring oppression.
2. *Break into scenes.* Teachers reflect on their personal experiences. First, they select a relevant situation and then script (alone or with a small group) a three-scene drama to perform with/for the others. Each drama will portray the oppressed person (the protagonist) and the person initially serving in the role of oppressor (the antagonist).
3. *Spect-acting.* As the antagonist and protagonist enact the scene, spect-actors can stop the action at any time, replace one of the actors, and improvise a new perspective, which is then interactionally validated, challenged, built upon, or refined.
4. *Is this real?* As multiple instances of spect-acting occur, there is a reality check process that clarifies the situation and the temperament and identity of both the protagonist and antagonist. This happens throughout the entire process.

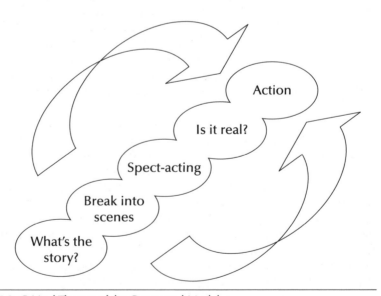

Figure 5.2. Critical Theater of the Oppressed Model
Source: Cahnmann-Taylor, Wooten, Souto-Manning, & Dice, 2009.

5. *Action.* In this last phase, there is collective and individual plotting of action, both on the individual and on the societal levels.

This process is not as linear as portrayed in the figure: There is frequent back-and-forth negotiation, and the five phases often overlap.

Throughout the book, we posit that Theatre of the Oppressed can serve as a tool to counter traditional forms of education oriented toward single-answer solutions and the teacher as isolated individual. As exemplified in the cases presented in this chapter, Forum Theatre may serve as a framework for critical performance, sensitivity and responsiveness to diversities, and positive change in teacher education. Like Boal, we believe that a description and enactment of power relations can reveal what may disable teachers in moments of communicative conflict in their professional lives. These may serve as tools to promote positive change.

Forum Theatre is built on the premise that there is no single and simple solution to conflict, but a gamut of perspectives and possible solutions. We understand that "the ways that people interact . . . depend on context—the frameworks for interpretation—that people bring to those experiences. . . . Context is itself a complex concept, whose meaning is not fixed" (Dyson & Genishi, 2005, p. 5). The context for learning moves toward embodied sites of practice where education is transitive—that is, the experiences of working teachers inform and influence teacher educators and vice versa. The collective practice of Theatre of the Oppressed via Forum Theatre becomes a rehearsal for real social action in teachers' lives.

The Forum Theatre process differs from role-playing because it is open-ended, with no definitive solution—instead, there is a multitude of possibilities. Forum Theatre is based on the process of problem-posing rather than problem solving at the onset. Edmond and Tilley (2007) explored how theatre goes beyond role-playing as it more fully explores contexts and interactional nuances. Theatre of the Oppressed, or, namely, Forum Theatre, goes beyond simple theatre in that it allows for the possibility of rendering multiple performances (and, therefore, behaviors) of the same episode that is generated from participating teachers' experiences.

In the following sections, we narrate cases of Forum Theatre, as we believe showing is better than telling. Although the cases we present are unique to the participants in our workshops, the process is one that can be extrapolated and used in any context—with participants who vary in age, status, and challenges but who share a common goal to activate, to further develop their abilities to promote change for a more just and democratic lived experience.

PERFORMING STRATEGIES FOR ACTION

In this section, we present two case studies of Forum Theatre. Marisol's and Sonia's cases both illustrate how participants perform problems and engage in dialogic options for action.

Marisol's Case

"Marisol," a pull-out ESOL teacher of Cuban origin, performed a recurring problem that she had with a colleague who often shopped online during instructional time, and appeared not to care about the ESOL students in her mainstream second-grade class. Marisol's oppressive situation resonated with other teachers' experiences with colleagues who were perceived as similarly unprofessional, disrespectful, or racist toward English language learners. For this reason, Marisol's story was chosen as a generative theme for collective engagement: how to be the most effective advocates for ESOL students among colleagues whose attitudes and actions were perceived to undermine advocacy and culturally responsive practices. The codification included participants verbally breaking the story into scenes—one scene between Marisol and her students, and two scenes between Marisol and her colleague, where the result was no change in the Protagonist Teacher's sense of dejection. The verbal script was dialectically negotiated by the group prior to spect-acting.

Marisol was the first to perform as the "Protagonist ESOL Teacher," and then described feeling frustrated and angry and wanting "to choke" her dismissive colleague [line 8], aware this was not a "real" option for resolving conflict. A peer teacher in the group, Jorge, wanted to suggest what Marisol might do to change her colleague's attitudes and/or behavior [lines 9–11]. In this performance-based focus group, telling someone "what to do" was insufficient. The Joker immediately directed Jorge to spect-act "as if" he were the ESOL teacher, performing his problem-posing strategy [line 10], and Jorge proceeded to do so [lines 11–16].

SCENE: SHOW, DON'T TELL

MARISOL: (*entering Mrs. Smith's room, where Mrs. Smith surfs the*   1
         Internet during instructional time, and tapping her softly on the
         shoulder) Hey.
MRS. SMITH: (*enthusiastically*) Oh, hi!   2
MARISOL: Hi. Um, I would like to take the children a little   3
         early today. Would you mind? I wanna order some pizza for
         them to celebrate how hard they've been working in class.

MRS. SMITH (Antagonist Teacher) (*looking away from her*   4
    computer and speaking to Marisol): Yes. Keep the ESOL kids,
    keep them *all*! (*spreads her hands away from her to emphasize* "all
    of the children")
MARISOL: Thank you. I will! (*hiding frustration*)   5
MRS. SMITH: Okay, great!   6
JOKER: Stop! (*to Marisol*) What are you feeling when she [the   7
    Antagonist] says that?
MARISOL: That I wanna *choke* her. (*laughter from group*)   8
    Because it's not like she's, like, "Oh *yeah*, someone is *doing*
    something good for them!" It's "*Thank God*, I don't have to *deal*
    with them, I don't even have to *look* at 'em."
JOKER: Does anyone have an idea, a strategy for change?   9
    Okay (*to Jorge*), you do? Replace Marisol.
(*Jorge hesitates, raises his hand to speak his idea.*)
JOKER: You, you need to *do* it. [See Figure 5.3.]   10
JORGE (*almost inaudibly in background*): Okay. (*Jorge rises   11
    to take over Marisol's "role" as the ESOL teacher.*)
(*Bell rings. Jorge, who has replaced Marisol, is standing in a corner of the
room in an imaginary doorway. "Mrs. Smith," the Antagonist Teacher,
now played by Debora, is typing with her back to him. Jorge walks up to
the teacher and addresses her.*)
JORGE (*as Marisol*): Hello, good morning, Mrs. Smith. I was   12
    wondering if I could have the ESOL students so I can take
    them on a special educational trip Friday?
MRS. SMITH: Please! Sure!   13
JORGE: Thank you. You know, I'd like to try a new activity   14
    with them, and I want to see what their reactions are. I'll be
    glad to let you know what they are. Would you like me to
    print it out or send it to you in an e-mail?
MRS. SMITH: Oh, whatever! Take 'em all!   15
JORGE: I'll be very glad to do that, and I'll let you know. I'll 16
    let Mrs. So-and-So also know what their reactions were.
    Thank you.
KARIN (*from audience*): Principal, whatever.   17
(*Laughter from group*)
JOKER: When you said Mrs. So-and-So, did you mean the   18
    principal?
JORGE: I meant an administrator.   19
JOKER: Okay. (*to the spect-actors*) Is this real?   20
MARISOL: No! This won't work because she will probably   21
    ask me at that point "What do you mean by telling So-and-So?"

Figure 5.3. Forum: Show, Don't Tell

I would just look like a tattletale. I really would. And what's the point? Everybody knows she doesn't teach, and nobody does anything! And this [Mrs. Smith] is a person that should know better (*furls her eyebrows, clenches her fists*). She used to be assistant principal until last year!

Jorge was one of many participating teachers who performed various strategies for communicating through this conflict, including everything from the practical (e.g., documenting the Antagonist's behavior, reporting the Antagonist's behavior to an administrator) to the ridiculous (e.g., destroying the Antagonist Teacher's computer to prevent her from shopping online and ignoring the ESOL students during instructional time). Despite solutions that didn't meet the reality check criteria for action, the more ridiculous strategies seemed to strengthen group identity and encourage more creative, out-of-the-box performances.

Although Marisol's story could have been easily explained and understood in words, a wholly verbal explanation would have lacked the visceral punch of her re-enactment with the Antagonist. Fellow spect-actors related to Marisol, perhaps not to the specifics of her case but rather because of the visible emotions of frustration brought forth by performing the life of the "idealistic new teacher" among cynical colleagues. Boal (1995) was adamant that replacing the Protagonist while spect-acting is not predicated on empathy, or being penetrated by the emotions of another, but rather on sympathy; that is, projecting one's own emotions on the scene and placing oneself in a situation that resonates with the spect-actor. Spect-actors are not "walking in the shoes" of the Protagonist, but rather are walking the same road as the Protagonist.

In several circumstances, a spect-actor spontaneously offered a verbal suggestion to the Protagonist, but when asked to embody the strategy in performance, the Protagonist declared that the suggestion didn't work because it didn't "feel right." This emphasis on feelings and the body became not only sites of enactment and credibility but also suggestions for change. In Marisol's case, one spect-actor stood uncomfortably close behind the seated mainstream teacher and peered over her shoulder at the computer screen, illustrating how body language may communicate disapproval in a safer and/or more effective way than spoken language.

Regardless of whether suggested strategies were deemed "real" or not, we've found that the process of reenactment itself promoted solidarity-building and was preparatory and agentive. Throughout various transcripts, we saw frequent bursts of laughter (such as the one above) expressed during group rehearsals. We've found laughter has served as a form of *dynamization*, arousing the group to "create new actions, new alternatives which are not substitutes for real action, but rehearsals, pre-actions . . . [for] a reality we are trying to change" (Boal, 1995, p. 72). Boal distinguished this kind of cathartic release of tension from the Aristotelian catharsis, which, he maintained, disempowers, tranquilizes, and dilutes the desire for change. In contrast, the group-generated laughter represented cathartic releases of tension through performance, having the potential to release spect-actors from detrimental blocks to change both in the performance and in real life.

Sonia's Case

Sonia, a pre-kindergarten teacher, presented a common problem in early childhood education—conflict between early childhood lead teachers and assistant teachers with varied professional experiences and educational credentials. Other K–12 teachers were present and collectively decided to focus on Sonia's narrative, which was representative of their own co-teaching experiences and therefore meaningful and useful to each of them (Jensen, 1999).

Sonia was frequently put down and challenged by the assistant teacher who had more seniority at the school where they worked. The more experienced assistant did not have the credentials to become a lead teacher, yet, according to Sonia, considered herself more knowledgeable about how best to teach young children and involve families. Sonia felt that the assistant teacher did not fulfill her duties, and that the assistant teacher undermined Sonia's authority in the classroom. Sonia tried confronting the assistant teacher and talking to the principal, but none of the solutions she tried yielded a satisfactory resolution. Sonia described the situation of recurring oppression:

> It all starts in the morning, when she comes in. The first thing: She comes in and goes to the computer and starts e-mailing. The kids are there and she just ignores them. When I ask her to help me, she compares me to the previous lead teachers. She intimidates me so much that I say only half the things I have to say. I want to say, "This is it." I gotta talk to her, but I can't. I even typed up the general job expectations for her: during this time I want you to do this and this and that. She just looked at me like, "What's the problem?"

As Sonia shared her struggle, delineating "What's the Story?", many of the participants were able to relate to the situation. Her dilemma was selected and broken into three scenes to be performed:

> *Scene 1.* The assistant teacher ignored Sonia's and the children's needs upon entry to the classroom.
> *Scene 2.* Sonia made a request to the assistant teacher for help.
> *Scene 3.* The assistant teacher compared Sonia to a previous teacher, seeking to exemplify how good teachers act.

As participating teachers engaged in spect-acting, members of the group suggested that Sonia change the way she presented herself when she interacted with her assistant teacher in order to convey a position of strength. Initially, when interacting with the assistant teacher, Sonia's diminutive posture slumped; she frowned and looked down at the floor. Her peers noticed that her soft voice and posture nonverbally positioned her as insecure, and nonagentive in the interaction. They encouraged her to speak louder, stand tall, and relax her facial muscles.

SCENE: BE A LION!

JOKER: I've noticed every time you perform talking to your colleague you've been doing this (*hunching shoulders forward and downward*).

SONIA [Protagonist Teacher]: Yeah, I know! I've been intimidated from the first day.

DORIS: Why don't you try putting your hand to, your hands up—make yourself higher? Your hands can help you go higher than she is [see Figure 5.4].

SONIA: Oh, really? I never heard of that—this is good, let's see if I can try that.

JOKER: That's what we say with mountain lions, too—if you see one on your path, don't run or crouch but rise up and make yourself bigger. Be a lion! Let's try it again.

Figure 5.4. Be a Lion!

Sonia: (*having second thoughts at acting it out on-the-spot*) I don't think I can do it.

Doris: You don't even have to put your hand up there, just feel like there's hair in your face and you move your hands to brush it away.

Sonia: (*motions her hands toward her face*) Oh, okay.

(*Group laughter*)

Upon spect-acting possibilities, Sonia immediately felt a difference. When Sonia considered "Is this Real?", many of the suggested actions (e.g., directly confronting the assistant teacher, reporting the assistant teacher's behaviors to the principal) were deemed unreal. Sonia ultimately was able to find some possible courses of action that could work in her context.

Action occurred in this case study through the lead teacher's subjective self-awareness, sense of empowerment, and taking action with new behaviors in the classroom. By acting out her experiences with the assistant teacher, Sonia realized that she had identified patterns of interaction (e.g., competition, bids for power and knowledge) that may have perpetuated the negative situation. The hierarchy established by the school district was seen as problematic by the assistant teacher who had more classroom experience but fewer professional credentials.

Confronting this issue and approaching an interaction with the assistant teacher was problematic and nerve-wracking for Sonia. Although the suggestion to merely change her body language was the only suggestion Sonia felt was realistic during the Forum, later, in a debriefing interview, she reflected on her experience in the group as helpful because it was less solution-focused and more process-oriented. She felt there was something she could do. She changed her own stance, something over which she had control. She also talked about returning to the focus group setting as a support structure to help monitor the progress of her situation.

Sonia: What do I do? I bring my problem there and act it out. I reveal myself, one layer after another, and just peel away the anxiety. I let other people have it, and we share our emotions and problems together. Sometimes you just don't need words; you just use your body language to let all the problems out (*laughs*). After each possibility, we act it out again until you feel comfortable with some of those solutions that can help you deal with the problem afterward. You feel better as you gradually solve the problem, or release it. At least, you release the intensity and tension of the conflict, and you do better and you learn from the process. It was actually empowering for me to see different ways to deal with the problems.

INTERVIEWER: What do you mean by *empowering*?

SONIA: Different people have different reactions and the same person may have different reactions as well if they take the time to rehearse. So, I need to open up and widen my view, and recognize that there might be a reason or reaction coming from my assistant teacher. She might not feel empowered. I know that if I see differently, say it differently, and act differently, I know that I can feel empowered by showing different body language. If I consider her situation, she might show a different side of her, too. Human beings have a lot of sides, a wide range of thinking, and respond differently to different actions. Now I know that. So, it was an empowering experience, recognizing the other's situation as I think of mine.

Regardless of the reality of any one specific solution to the situation presented, Sonia articulated the need to consider the multiple facets of the person with whom she was in conflict (see Chapter 6 for more on the multiple facets, or "Rainbow of Desire," influencing one's discourses and actions). This sense of having rehearsed options for changing the situation (even if in small ways) served to reduce stress in a situation that might otherwise have been oppressive.

CHANGING SCRIPTS IN REAL LIVES

As part of our work in Forum Theatre, we have engaged in obtaining feedback from teacher-participants about their experiences, and we highly recommend the use of evaluations to serve a teacher-educator's iterative cycle of planning, teaching, and reflecting. Over a period of 6 years, in anonymous evaluations, participants commented on their engagement and pleasure in this new form of professional development. In Likert scale surveys, 68% of attendees classified Forum Theatre sessions as "very useful" for professional development, 32% deemed them "useful," with no participant rating the experience below a "4" on a 1–5 scale. Many praised the performance work in contrast to seat- and text-based work more customary in teacher education environments. Following is a representative example from anonymous evaluations:

Problems and situations [enacted] were directly relevant to real classroom happenings, and they were very useful to cope with real problems if they arise later. *This is something that the classes don't teach in the coursework, but every teacher faces these conflicts* (italics added).

In addition to written evaluations, we also conducted interviews. According to the interview data, this process was helpful not only to the particular person who shared the situation, but to others as well, as they employed Forum Theatre as a tool to deal with conflict and oppression. As a result of this process, we have seen instances of change at the personal level (e.g., "I can deal with this," "I feel so much better") and at the contextual level (e.g., "I changed schools," "I talked to the principal"). Although change is not always immediate, according to debriefing interviews, it seems to happen socioemotionally (affecting how participants felt about the situation) as well as tangibly (expanding the repertoire of instruments or tools available to do something about changing the situation). More about this will be discussed in the Conclusion.

FACILITATING THE PROCESS: FORUM THEATRE AS FOUNDATIONAL FOR PROFESSIONAL DEVELOPMENT

After engaging in this process multiple times over 6 years, we have gained insights into the possibilities and obstacles. We offer some of our learnings as a way to facilitate the implementation of Forum Theatre in your context.

Although the optimum way to facilitate/difficultate the Forum Theatre process is to spend time generating and sharing each individual's personal challenges and then deciding as a group to focus on one, for various reasons, this may not be desirable or feasible. Time is a constant constraint and generating everyone's stories and choosing among them can be very lengthy and present difficult choices. Additionally, participants can be hesitant to reveal their struggles, especially if the group hasn't spent much vulnerable time together. Based on our experience, we have been able to codify the varying kinds of struggles in which teachers are likely to engage. When we are short on time or new to a group but want to engage students in discussing the gritty details of the teaching life, we draw on a rich cache of teacher stories to lay the groundwork for a session of Forum Theatre. To facilitate this process, we share two methods that may be useful to you: *trans/scripting* and *vignettes*.

Trans/scripting

When we hear a case like Marisol's or Sonia's, concerning struggles with more jaded, even racist colleagues, one approach to record this material has been to create what we call "trans/scripts" (Cahnmann-Taylor, Wooten, Souto-Manning, & Dice, 2009). Trans/scripts emerge from original transcripts of audio-recorded Forum sessions. As artful researchers and teacher educators, we compress and dramatize the original discourse into scripts that resemble short plays. These can then be shared with other groups of teachers as "learning cases" to be reimagined and re-enacted together. Trans/scripts are particularly useful in a single session or in visiting workshops where time is a constraint. Below is a trans/script we created from Marisol's story (told above). Such trans/scripts help make teacher stories portable and expand the dialogue from one local context to another.

Trans/script: Marisol's Case— *"With colleagues like this, who needs enemies?"*

SCENE 1. WHAT ARE YOU DOING IN CLASS?

Marisol Jiménez is with her second-grade ESOL students, ready to take them back to their homeroom teacher. She engages Angel in discussion.

MS. JIMÉNEZ: (*to the class*) Children, let's get ready to go back to class. Tell me, Angel, what are you learning in Mrs. Smith's classroom?
ANGEL: *Nada.*
MS. JIMÉNEZ: What do you mean *nada*? Nothing? You must be learning *some*thing.
ANGEL: Ms. Jiménez, we don't learn in that class. Mrs. Smith just sits there all day at her computer (*mimics typing on a keyboard*).

SCENE 2. NOT EVEN HELLO

Ms. Jiménez takes her students back to class. She stands at the door to Mrs. Smith's classroom and waits to engage her. Mrs. Smith doesn't look up from her computer. Ms. Jiménez feels dejected and leaves the room without engaging her colleague.

SCENE 3. TAKE THEM! TAKE THEM ALL!

Ms. Jiménez returns the next day to Mrs. Smith's classroom and tries to get her attention. After several seconds, Mrs. Smith finally looks up from her monitor.

MS. JIMÉNEZ: (*to Mrs. Smith*) Good morning.
MRS. SMITH: Oh, is it a good morning? A good morning is the crossword and a refillable cup of coffee! (*laughs and turns back to her screen*)

Ms. Jiménez: Mrs. Smith, my students have made a lot of progress
in reading and I'd like to celebrate this week with a pizza
party. I was wondering if it'd be all right to keep them through
lunch this Friday?

Mrs. Smith: Keep them? You want them on Friday, *keep* them,
keep them *all!* All day if you want, no problem with me.

Ms. Jiménez: Thank you. (*leaves the room dejected, angry, and feeling
isolated*)

Trans/scripts become both product and process, used and re-scripted with
groups of teachers in different contexts for addressing tensions and strategies critical multicultural educators employ in the midst of conflict and
social change.

Vignettes

In addition to trans/scripts, we have also used open-ended vignettes (see
Figure 5.5) based on generative themes—encouraging participating teachers to trans/script their own scenes based on real-life connections. Below
is one such vignette that has appealed to groups of educators in a wide
range of grade levels and subject areas.

Figure 5.5. Posters of Vignettes

Open-ended Vignette: "You are nobody"— Working with a Student Who Doesn't Respect Your Authority

I am disheartened after working with a student who continuously misbehaves and disrupts my elementary school class. Despite several administrative interventions, the student is still giving me problems. When I try to reprimand him, he says, "You are nobody. My mom can come in here and say anything she wants." I don't feel like I have the skills to handle him, and I am exhausted by the power struggles in my classroom.

We provided this vignette to a group of 23 teachers. The teachers worked in smaller groups of three or four to create unique versions of this commonly experienced tension regarding student participation and behavior. Each group's performance became a new trans/script for generating new possibilities for action. This allows for the process to be facilitated (although not compromised) in light of time and space boundaries (Larson & Marsh, 2005).

In Figure 5.6, we share a compilation of vignettes used with foreign language teachers during a 3-hour workshop (Wooten & Cahnmann-Taylor, 2007). These and other stories may be adapted and transformed for local needs, and may serve as examples and help generate participating teachers' own stories.

Most teacher educators are familiar with the varying kinds of concerns that teachers in many different curricular areas raise in regard to their professional lives and the scope of antagonists who enter the room. We suggest building your own rich collection of stories and putting them forward as dynamic "texts" to be rehearsed, debated, revised, and researched.

ART TAKES TIME, BUT TIME IS SHORT

Overall, our experiences with Forum Theatre have been meaningful and exhilarating, and we continually seek ways to infuse this technique into our courses, workshops, and presentations. But to quote Benjamin Franklin's riff on *Ars longa, vita brevis*, "Art is long and time is short" (in Sizer, 1973, p. 56). Teachers and teacher educators are always pressed for time: There is always more to do, more curriculum to prepare, new methodologies, disciplinary procedures, paperwork, and so forth. To engage in theatre practices is to engage in art, which requires some degree of time and leisure. Wrestling with this tension, we have found ways to adapt Forum

Circle the situations that you relate to and put a star by the one that you MOST identify with. There is also room below to sketch out your own story.

1. Lacking Motivation

I'm a 9th-grade French teacher working in an urban high school in Chicago. I believe it's best to use as much of the target language as possible and aim to teach new material through French—introducing vocabulary and grammar through cultural lessons of interest to my students. Many of my students sleep through the entire class, and when asked a question, remain silent or goof off, encouraging their peers to laugh and waste class time. One student left my class the other day and mumbled, "Why do I have to study French anyhow, this class is a bunch of b.s.!" I was horrified. What do I do to get them interested in studying French?

2. Stereotypes

I teach Spanish to middle school students. One of my students said she was interested in Spanish so she'd know how to tell the landscapers how to mow her lawn—she said this and smirked. I believe my students have highly stereotypical and racist attitudes toward Spanish speakers. What do I do when students make comments that make dangerous assumptions about the Spanish-speaking populations in the United States?

3. Who Can Teach?

I teach high school Spanish. Last week, one of my students asked me if I was Hispanic. I said I wasn't, but I love teaching the Spanish language and its cultures. Another student quickly responded that he had thought I was a "real" Hispanic and asked me why he should learn Spanish from a "fake." I was completely caught off-guard. What can I say when there are many times I don't know how to say something in Spanish, and students make it clear they see me as Hispanic and then distrust my expertise to teach Spanish when I say I'm not?

4. I'll Never Learn

Recently, a student in my German class failed her second exam. I had a meeting with her after school where she explained she was very bad at languages and asked if she could have alternative assignments so she could pass this required course. What do I say to students who assume they are "bad" at learning languages? How do I combat this misperception that one is innately good or bad at language acquisition?

5. Foreign Language Isn't Important

I'm the only foreign language teacher in my high school in a rural area in the South. I attend faculty meetings where my colleagues make remarks that devalue what I do in the classroom. In a recent discussion of testing, one colleague turned to me and said how lucky I was that I didn't have to feel the heat because no one was looking at foreign language performance. She made other comments about how "easy" my job must be compared to those teaching content matter like English and math. I was stunned, silent, offended. What could I have said?

Figure 5.6. Challenges Foreign Language Teachers Face

Source: Wooten & Cahnmann-Taylor, 2007.

Theatre to make the most use of time. We hope this chapter provides a rich overview of what is possible—the depth of conversation and debate that can take place when teachers such as Marisol and Sonia share their pressing and urgent struggles in the profession. We also hope that our ideas for efficient use of time, including the use of vignettes and trans/scripts, make this process more likely to be practiced, even within the constraints of a single session with a new group. We encourage improvisation and (re)design for situated contexts and local needs—and we hope you'll tell us about your innovations!

Troubling Oppressions, Seeking Change:
Rainbow of Desire, Invisible, and Legislative Theatre

IN THIS CHAPTER, we present three techniques that may be useful to teachers and teacher educators who want to trouble oppression and embrace transformation in their immediate contexts and beyond. Through Rainbow of Desire, we challenge the idea of oppressor-oppressed identities as fixed and unchangeable. We show how teachers came to reconceptualize behaviors as they sought to understand the many hues of a person's behaviors and actions. We also explore the possibilities of Invisible Theatre and Legislative Theatre for raising awareness, promoting change, and igniting transformation in societal as well as legislative contexts.

SOMEWHERE OVER THE RAINBOW: THE MANY SHADES OF TEACHING AND RAINBOW OF DESIRE TECHNIQUES

The basis of Forum Theatre in Chapter 5 asks teachers to think of themselves as the protagonists of their own lives and to collectively rehearse strategies for working with and through antagonists and antagonisms. We believe that teachers need experience rehearsing their own agentive stances, to understand their options in moments of conflict, and to be able to teach and model this practice with students.

We also believe that conflict has many origins, often quite distant from the parameters of an initial encounter. Although we strongly encourage the practice of Forum Theatre in teacher preparation, we also see the limitations inherent in strategies that focus on static and one-dimensional identities where the teacher always plays the role of the "good person" against external forces of evil. While the practice of identifying clear-cut heroes and villains works well in movies depicting teachers' lives (such as *Stand and Deliver* starring Edward James Olmos, *Dangerous Minds* starring Michelle Pfeiffer, or *Dead Poets Society* starring Robin Williams), there is rarely a clear-cut good or bad guy in the real context of the U.S. education system. In reality, our identities and interactions with others are informed and constrained by multiple motivations and sources, diverse and overlapping social, cultural, and status positions in terms of race, class, gender, religion, and so forth. Might a teacher be considered by one parent, student, or administrator, as "the hero" while simultaneously being perceived by another as "the enemy"? Absolutely! Might teachers feel oppressed by their administrators and at the same time be positioned as oppressors by parents and/or coworkers? Yes! This is why clear-cut personifications of oppressor and oppressed, of antagonist and protagonist, are, at best, incomplete. Rainbow of Desire allowed us to extrapolate such fixed constructs and embrace the dynamism of conflict and/in teaching.

Teachers, students, parents, administrators, professors, paraprofessionals, and politicians, like all human beings, are complicated and multifaceted, and rarely all good or all bad. Beyond Forum Theatre, we need additional strategies to illuminate nuances of character and how we perform ourselves in everyday life (Goffman, 1959). We find that Augusto Boal's (1995) work, *Rainbow of Desire*, provides just the techniques needed to explore how each individual can embody multiple subjectivities and reveal the dynamism and fluidity of human nature. Central to this technique is the notion of the rainbow—that any one individual embodies multiple "hues" that color our past experience and moment-to-moment communication and what we perceive as possible for future action. Uncovering the multiple colors that inform any interactional moment allows teachers to see fluidity and possibility in every encounter and to model these options for students working in ever more diverse contexts.

Originally, Boal (1995) complicated Forum Theatre when he was forced to move his work from South America to European contexts due to his exile from Brazil. As discussed in Chapter 2, Boal's techniques originated in the context of overt abuses of power in regard to intolerable working conditions and an oppressive police state. Upon changing contexts to Lisbon and Paris, such power relationships remained, although in a more covert manner. To adapt to these new contexts while continuing his work to represent and reenvision oppression, he encountered other forms of internal oppression more common in democracies such as "loneliness" and the "impossibility of communicating with others" (Boal, 1995, p. 8). Thus, he shifted theatre techniques from those focusing on the antagonist "cops in the street" to antagonists that are often more emotionally internal, and which he referred to as the "cops in the head." He wrote:

> The cops are in our heads, but their headquarters and barracks must be on the outside. The task was to discover how these "cops" got into our heads, and to invent ways of dislodging them. . . . Throughout the last few years I have continued to work on this aspect of the *Theatre of the Oppressed*, this superposition of fields: the theatrical and the therapeutic (p. 8).

Getting to know the "cops" required a "therapeutic" theatrical approach, one that would illuminate the multiple voices and influences that drive any one person's motivations and actions—those of the antagonist and protagonist in real-time interaction. Take, for example, Marisol, the ESOL teacher whose case was described in Chapter 5 in relation to her mainstream teacher colleague, "Mrs. Smith." What are the different emotions and motivations that drive each of their performances as colleagues in the same professional context? If we complicate the character of "Mrs. Smith," what aspects of her own experience and social context might contribute to what Marisol perceived as racist behavior? How can we get to know and understand our antagonists, even when they appear to be from very different backgrounds in terms of race, class, country of origin, and religion, among other possible differences? Likewise, how can we better understand our own motivations in order to honor the complexity involved when different, often contrary, perspectives come into play? How can we develop our understanding in order to better serve our students, cultivating an environment that is welcoming rather than hostile to differences in opinion, cultures, histories, and desires?

HOW RAINBOW OF DESIRE TAKES PLACE

Just as it takes a prism to reveal all the colors within what appears to be colorless sunlight, so too the complex hues of one's person require a prism to reveal their complexity. Rainbow of Desire techniques function like light through drops of water, helping to reveal to us the various hues of humanity that are always present but are seldom visible on the surface. Rainbow of Desire techniques build on what has come before in Image and Forum Theatre, where characters in conflict have been established—the teacher in the workroom with her colleague; the teacher in a parent-teacher conference; the teacher in a weekend graduate class; and so on.

Understanding the Antagonist

Take, for example, Danielle, a drama teacher who found great satisfaction and progress when working with students deemed as "the lowest-performing students in the school." When the school principal told her she could no longer work with "underachievers" and would be restricted to taking only the "best students" out of the class, Danielle was disappointed and angry. Danielle felt restricted from reaching the students who needed her most. We encouraged the group to dig deep into the Rainbow of Desire to discover what was influencing the principal's feelings and actions. Each member of the troupe was invited to the stage to act out different aspects of the principal, providing a sentence or phrase and a physical motion:

> MONA: (*stoops tenderly over the teacher, motioning with her hand as if petting a cat or rocking a cradle*) She's so young and naive.
>
> RICHARD: (*sweeping outward with his right arm*) I used to *be* that person.
>
> JOKER: Good. Next one. You're *all* the principal. Someone, add another layer.
>
> DANIELLE: (*clutching her head as if she is discouraged and has a migraine*) I'm *so* tired of numbers.
>
> JILL: (*standing straight up with her arms folded across her chest*) This is *my* domain.
>
> MARY: (*lies on her back on the floor and curls up with her knees crossed and pulled into her chest, arms clasped around her knees, rocking back and forth.*) I used to be a baby.
>
> JOKER: Okay, somebody, somebody else add. What's missing? Who else is this person?
>
> KAVITHA: (*clasping and unclasping her hands in front of her*) How do I get the standards met? How do I get all the requirements met?

JOKER: Good. What else? (*points to Melanie*)
MELANIE: (*grabbing her middle*) I'm so frustrated; I think I'm going
to throw up.

Although the drama teacher was the story's protagonist, the group
performed multiple dimensions of the perceived antagonist, the principal,
to understand her as more fully human, someone who also struggled with
being a part of an oppressive system and also felt frustrated working within
that system's constraints (e.g. "I'm so tired of numbers"; "How do I get
the standards met?"). By playing the antagonistic character, one gains
insight into how to work with this character, developing new strategies
that can emerge from compassion.

Exploring the Protagonist's Emotions

Rainbow of Desire can also work as a technique to follow Forum Theatre.
Consequently, it serves to further complicate the situation and considers
multiple perspectives and positionings across time and space. For example,
in the following case, spect-actors started off with Forum Theatre and rehearsed three scenes regarding a conflict between a teacher, Roberta Salas,
and a rebellious student, Dana. We found this to be a very common situation, a constant power struggle for many of the teachers with whom we've
worked. Because of this, we spent considerable time encouraging spect-actors
to intervene and change an aspect of the protagonist teacher's behavior that
might also influence Dana's response and participation. Further, because
many teachers could closely and directly relate to the situation, some deemed
the solution presented to be real, while others did not. Thus there were a
variety of perspectives offered. Following is a trans/script of the three scenes:

SCENE 1. WHAT DO YOU MEAN YOU DIDN'T DO IT?

Roberta Salas is with her fourth-grade students, checking homework assignments.

Ms. SALAS: (*to the class*) Children, take out your homework. (*in
front of first student's desk*) Very good, Iliana, you're making
progress. (*continues praising others*) Very good. Thank you, very
good. Yes, excellent.
Ms. SALAS: (*stops in front of Dana's desk*) Dana, where's your work?
DANA: (*shrugs her shoulders*) I didn't do it.
Ms. SALAS: What do you mean you didn't do it? Why not?
DANA: I didn't feel like it, that's why (*turns toward her neighbor to talk*).

SCENE 2. TO THE PRINCIPAL'S OFFICE!

MS. SALAS: Dana, we've been going through this all year long. It's not acceptable for you not to do your homework and not to respect this classroom. We're going to the principal right now.

DANA: Fine, what do I care? [See Figure 6.1.]

CLASSMATES: Oooooohhhhhhh!

SCENE 3. NOT THE DESIRED OUTCOME.

MS. SALAS: (*Exits the principal's office and meets Dana, seated outside*) Dana, I just spoke with the principal, and we called your mother. We've decided to give you a suspension for 3 days.

DANA: YES!!! (*pumps her arm with enthusiasm*)

In order to deepen our understanding of the teacher's role and perceived options, we combined Forum Theatre with Rainbow of Desire techniques, exploring the many different emotions and feelings a teacher may have during a conflict with a student like Dana. Clearly, in the transcript above, the teacher perceived the student as performing oppressive actions

Figure 6.1. Trans/script #1: Fine, What Do I Care?

and attitudes, nevertheless she herself was holding power over Dana. These were issues that needed to be addressed beyond what was possible with Forum Theatre, so we decided to transition to Rainbow. Employing both techniques can offer hopeful possibilities to situations such as the one illustrated above. According to the Brecht Forum (2009):

> The merging of these two techniques, Rainbow of Desire and Forum Theatre, provides an innovative approach to telling stories about conflict and oppression: stories that are generated through the use of Rainbow of Desire are then developed as Forum Theatre skits. In this way, each technique enhances the other and gives participants more tools for exploring strategies to use in resolving conditions of oppression. (¶ 2)

In the case above, determining who was the "oppressor" and who was the "oppressed" seemed unclear; it was interchangeable according to particular points of view. In fact, both parties may have felt they were simultaneously oppressing and oppressed. In response to the three scenes above, spect-actors were encouraged one by one to join an ensemble of human sculptures portraying the many hues of "Ms. Roberta Salas" when interacting with disrespectful students like "Dana." The following transcript and Figure 6.2 illustrate what took place next:

Figure 6.2. Rainbow of Desire

JOKER: We're going to do what Boal calls Rainbow of Desire. The idea is that we need to understand the complexity of our characters. There are multiple behaviors, emotions, and histories that inform the present moment. Please come up, one volunteer at a time. What is that teacher, Ms. Salas, feeling? Sculpt a silent image that would express it. (*Rona comes onto the stage and performs strangling Dana.*)

JOKER: Freeze. That's one (*laughter from some in the group*). Someone else?

ROBERTA: Yeah (*poses with her hands in the air like she's had enough*). I'm frustrated (*points to herself*), completely frustrated.

JOKER: Good, another!

LISETTE: (*sits in the seat next to Dana, leans over so that her right ear is near Dana's chest*) I'm trying to listen to what's in her heart.

SPECTACTORS: Yes! Yes!

LINDA: (*lies down on the floor at the edge of the audience*) So can I stay over here 'cuz I'm home?

JOKER: Sure! (*nodding to Linda*)

LINDA: I'm sleeping and I'm dreaming. I'm waking up, and I'm trying to figure out how to solve the problem in my sleep (*As she speaks, she rises to a sitting position with right hand to chin—in a pondering gesture.*)

ANGELA: That happens to me, too!

SPECTACTORS: (*General agreement*)

RONA: (*Lowers hands from chokehold.*) I want to say something. "I'm not going to choke the child if they do this" to me. And they *do* do this to me sometimes. I mean what you *do* and what you *feel* are two different things.

As Boal designed it, Theatre of the Oppressed (including Forum Theatre, Rainbow of Desire, and other T.O. techniques) opened up a space for critical, performative pedagogy and embraced a language of possibility as participants engaged theatrically in contexts where the qualities of the protagonist and antagonist were multifaceted and contextually situated. Just as Rona stated (above), what we *do* and what we *feel* are often very different. Although there are several approaches to teacher education that espouse "reflective teaching," these are often very individual processes whereby a novice teacher reflects in isolation through a journal or in paired collaborations with a mentor teacher or university supervisor. Furthermore, one's perceptions and practices are often uneven, as many studies have documented discrepancies between self-reported and observational data of a teacher's actions. According to Logan, DiCintio, Cox, and Turner

(1995), teachers' self-reported practices align with their beliefs more closely than with their actual practices. Thus, it becomes important to step aside and analyze the complexity of situations, including the roles teachers play in covert and overt ways, becoming aware of some of the oppressions perpetrated by their very practices.

Verbalizing Silence

One of the teachers participating in our workshops offered the story of her recurring struggle with African American students who made derogatory comments about Latinos in her racially diverse high school social studies class. Again and again, Latinos were stereotyped and profiled by African American students (the reverse was also true). As several participants seemed dismayed by the passive, victim response of one Latina in the class, we stopped the Forum Theatre process and asked participants to enter the Latina student's "Rainbow of Desire," as thoughts are often not verbalized. Disturbing the idea of silence as passivity, we asked participating teachers to step into the Latina student's shoes. What would she be thinking? What might be the voices behind a Latina/o student's silence? Some teachers offered the following voices:

> José: (*chest puffed out*) Qué te pasa, cabrón? [What's up, asshole?]
> Alona: (*scowl on her face*) Screw you. What do you know about me?
> Alex: What? What did you say? I thought Latinos and African Americans were on the same side!
> Liliana: (*pulling up a chair and slouching in it*) I don't want to be here.
> Liz: (*on her knees with her head bowed*) Lord, they just don't understand.
> Kelly: I can't believe the ignorance that I have to put up with here. You know, the ignorance is abhorrent. I wish that the teacher would address this.
> Clarissa: This is full of fooling. I don't know why I have to put up with this.
> Monika: (*kneels with arms crossed*) That comment doesn't pertain to me. I'm just like everybody else.

Again and again, we found that teachers appreciated opportunities to slow down time and critically examine the charged moments that took place in their classrooms. Sometimes a silence might mean passivity ("That comment doesn't pertain to me"); other instances might mean outrage ("Screw you. What do you know about me?"). There is truly a rainbow of possibilities. Taking the time to collectively explore the rainbow of responses proved to be valuable for participating teachers. When asked about their responses to Rainbow of Desire, Kelly, Clarissa, and Carla responded in the following manner:

KELLY: It's a powerful tool.

JOKER: Why?

KELLY: I like it a lot because for the longest time I stayed stuck in Maria's [the Latina student's] silent response. That's how I saw her—as the crying victim. I didn't see that there was an array of possible responses for her. Even when I see her in the hallway, that's all I continue to see in her. Before this exercise, I didn't recognize that she has many voices and that "the victim" was only one voice in one moment under one circumstance. It's important to recognize that she's a woman of many voices and that she selected a particular voice in that moment based on those circumstances. So I like the fact that there are so many possible options for her.

CLARISSA: I think maybe an exercise like that is providing different responses. Sometimes we get trapped in our own little way of responding, and a classroom environment can be a place to share different ways. I mean, if you can actually talk about how we feel when a racist comment like that is made or we can do an exercise like that together in the classroom, that's great. Okay, I can say to my students: Let's, you know, let's act this out.

CARLA: For me, the exercise tells me that maybe it wasn't just her. The comment also affected many others who didn't react at all but who internally have reacted in all those different ways. As a teacher, if you see one person crying, you may think it's just one person in the class who's hurt, but there might be more than one.

Recognizing the Benefits of Rainbow of Desire

Participating teachers unequivocally saw the benefits of slowing down and considering possibilities as opposed to making assumptions that may or may not have been correct, but at times were taken at face value (Ochs & Capps, 2001). However, as a passing moment was happening, there was seldom time to consider multiple perspectives and possibilities. In the blink of an eye decisions need to be made—or do they? Rainbow of Desire allowed teachers to rethink concepts of time and roles in the classroom. It may be more beneficial to take the time to fully understand situations than to act immediately on what could end up being a big misunderstanding. Or, it may be wiser to blur the roles and boundaries in the classroom, so that the teacher is not positioned as the "know it all" person. Rainbow strengthened the case for dialectically negotiated authority and the true need to embrace the blurring of teacher and learner roles (Freire, 1970). Really, how many times do teachers act as if they know it all while at the same time realizing that the opposite is true?

Although stepping back and acting out in order to perform their lives and change the world are necessary steps, seldom are creative methodologies such as theatre available for new teachers, especially those who are working on behalf of traditionally marginalized communities. Nevertheless, our experience working with teachers pointed toward the need to engage teachers in re-enacting their experiences in a collective way, rehearsing and validating the emotional hues that inform embodied practice. Rainbow of Desire is a terrific technique to use when discussing real-life conflicts in teachers' lives, in students' experiences, or even in the context of discussing literary characters as the technique can help students and teachers examine the complexities of living in so-called democratic societies and teaching in diverse schools.

In addition to Rainbow of Desire, Boal presented techniques that embrace political, collective action, going beyond the walls of schools, seeking to impact and make a difference in society at large. In the next sections, we briefly describe Invisible Theatre and Legislative Theatre, which take the next step to political, collective action. Although we have not yet engaged in these with the teachers, we present them here because we recognize the importance of and interconnectedness between schools and society.

INVISIBLE THEATRE: MAKING THE INVISIBLE VISIBLE

Invisible Theatre (Boal, 1979) is a way of performing to raise awareness of social issues, to name oppression. As Freire (1970) proposed, the first step toward change and transformation is awareness of what is happening. So often in our lives, we take things for granted. We come to accept them for what they are and not for what they *could* be. To break the routine of our everyday lives and make people aware of issues that could be transformed for the betterment of an individual group or society as a whole, Invisible Theatre may be used as a tool.

As explained in Chapter 2, Invisible Theatre often happens in places where a performance would not ordinarily take place—in the streets, in a market, in a restaurant, or in a shopping center. Invisible Theatre is comprised of a rehearsed, theatrical performance that is performed outside of the theatre, in real life, centering on oppression and social issues. In the truest sense, spectators enact roles according to their beliefs, as they are not aware of the theatrical nature of the performance—they believe it to be real. Boal (1979) posited:

> It is always very important that the actors do not reveal themselves to be actors! On this rests the *invisible* nature of this form of theatre. And it is precisely this invisible quality that will make the spectator act freely and fully, as if he were living a real situation—and after all, it is a real situation! (pp. 146–147)

The actors do not know who the audience will be and how they will react, but they may try to ascertain predictions as they rehearse their performance. Nevertheless, Invisible Theatre is performed in public and witnessed by unexpected bystanders whom the actors will try to get unknowingly involved in the scene. According to Boal (1979), "the people who are near become involved in the eruption [of the theatre] and the effects of it last long after the skit is ended" (p. 144). Invisible Theatre has been called "free theatre" because formalities (along with other constraining components of traditional theatre) are left aside and "the theatrical energy is completely liberated" (p. 147).

Although we have not yet engaged teachers in Invisible Theatre, we acknowledge the power of such a strategy to raise awareness of educational issues, such as NCLB, involving those who would otherwise not be closely vested or well informed. The box below illustrates one way in which Invisible Theatre was used by Augusto Boal in Peru. The specific event/example described below took place at the Carmen Market, in Comas (about 10 miles from downtown Lima). It was documented by Augusto Boal in *Theatre of the Oppressed* (1979). Hopefully, as the situated representation of a phenomenon, it can shed light onto the power of such a method to involve those who would otherwise be bystanders in getting involved and advocating for important issues.

> Two actresses were protagonists in a scene enacted at a vegetable stand. One of them, who was pretending to be illiterate, insisted that the vendor was cheating her, taking advantage of the fact that she did not know how to read; the other actress checked the figures, finding them to be correct, and advised the "illiterate" one to register in one of the ALFIN literacy courses. After some discussion about the best age to start one's studies, about what to study and with whom, the first actress kept on insisting that she was too old for those things. It was then that a little old woman, leaning on her cane, very indignantly shouted:

"My dears, that's not true! For learning and making love one is never too old!"

Everyone witnessing the scene broke into laughter at the old woman's amorous outburst, and the actresses were unable to continue the scene. (Boal, 1979, p. 147)

The scene above clearly sought to raise awareness of how individuals could have access to adult literacy programs offered through Operacíon Alfabetizacíon Integral (ALFIN). Although this was the intended aim, the market bystander also raised issues regarding ageism in terms of learning and making love. As observed here, Invisible Theatre proved a powerful tool to raise awareness and to value common people's voices, opinions, and oppressions in authentic ways.

LEGISLATIVE THEATRE: THEATRE AS POLITICS AND DEMOCRACY AS THEATRE

Although we acknowledge the need to raise awareness to promote change, in so-called democratic societies with an organized government, one must aim to affect policy in order to promote transformation on a wider scale. With the objective of not only raising individual, collective, and social awareness of the issues oppressing individuals and communities, Boal created Legislative Theatre, which specifically aims to promote transformation at the policy level. As we described in Chapter 2, Legislative Theatre emerged in 1992 as Boal, an elected city council member, attempted to connect people's real issues and oppressions to the decision-making, policy process in Rio de Janeiro. Legislative Theatre challenges the idea of the elector as "a mere spectator to the actions of the parliamentarian" (Boal, 1998, p. 16). According to Boal, the aim of Legislative Theatre is

> to bring the theatre back to the heart of the city, to produce not catharsis, but dynamization. Its objective is not to pacify its audiences, to tranquilise them, to return them to a state of equilibrium and acceptance of society as it is, but, again, contrarily, to develop their desire for change. The *Theatre of the Oppressed* seeks not only to develop this desire but to create a space in which it can be stimulated and experienced, and where future actions arising from it can be rehearsed. The Legislative Theatre seeks to go further and to transform that desire into law. (We must be aware that law is always someone's desire—it is always the desire of the powerful: let's democratize this desire, let's make our desire become law too!)

Legislative Theatre is a form of politics that is transitive—it proposes dialogue, interaction, change. It offers a systematic and organized effort to link practice to policy in ways that may be transformative to education in the United States. Although neither of us has taken this up yet, we can imagine both Invisible and Legislative Theatre as the logical next steps toward transforming teachers' stories into political action, thereby engaging in "theatre as transitive democracy" (Boal, 1998, p. 18).

Implications Across Contexts

J̲U̲S̲T̲ ̲A̲S̲ ̲W̲E̲ ̲B̲E̲L̲I̲E̲V̲E̲ teachers benefit from revisiting their classroom experiences through performance, thus becoming critically aware of emergent patterns and possibilities for change, so too we believe teacher educators benefit from such critical reflection. In addition to opportunities to bring our own concerns to theatre workshops with other teacher educators, we also use research as a tool for revisiting and critically reflecting on our own practice.

As we explained earlier, we have been practicing Theatre of the Oppressed activities for several years with a growing cohort of teachers. We have asked participating teachers to allow us to audio- and video-record these sessions so we could analyze what took place, identify emergent themes, and consider the implications of this practice both for ourselves and for teacher educators in general. After our workshops, we asked participating teachers to complete anonymous surveys to evaluate what took place and to volunteer for longer interviews to further elicit their reactions to this practice as well as its short- and longer-term benefits. Although not all participants were immediately comfortable with a camera in the workshop space, we aimed to cultivate an environment where all participants knew that our empirical and pedagogical goals were to honor their experiences and help us grow as a community of critically reflective practitioners. Sonia, a workshop participant from the very beginning of our project, summed up her experience:

> I didn't know about drama, and I don't feel comfortable acting out situations. I'm kind of *shy*, and it's *hard* to do anything in front of other people. And then somebody was gonna watch me and record me! But I had a great time. In the beginning I felt shy to act, but I liked it afterward. Sometimes you have built-up emotions, and then, with the encouragement of a supportive group, you can just let it out, one layer after another layer. And suddenly you feel like a different person! You see different ways to deal with the situation. It was great.

In examining our data, we asked what kinds of patterns have emerged when teachers perform "different ways to deal with the situation[s]" that concern them in their professional lives. We have been surprised to see that from group to group, context to context, teachers often proposed similar types of interventions during Forum Theatre rehearsals; likewise, we were struck by the diversity, humor, and creativity with which individuals addressed similar scenarios. We review these strategies in order to highlight patterns and surprises that emerged when teachers Acted Up! in our study.

CALLS TO AUTHORITY AND DOCUMENTATION

One of the most often-repeated solutions to teachers' struggles with parents, teachers, paraprofessionals, students, and others was a *call to authority*, performing ways the protagonist teacher might seek allies with those who have power over the antagonist in question. A related strategy, *documentation*, also recurred regularly, where spect-actors would suggest keeping overt or covert files regarding antagonists' inappropriate behavior, in order to report this behavior to an authority figure with power to change the situation. One such example was portrayed in Sonia's case where, as a novice teacher, she struggled with the person placed in her classroom to be an assistant but whose actions appeared to undermine Sonia's authority. Workshop participants enacted calling the principal for an observation, secretly videotaping class activity, and keeping a dated log of any instances of tardiness or other unprofessional behavior the assistant exhibited.

Analyzing all three of these spect-acting possibilities, participating teachers explained that these covert tactics may appear useful at first but, in reality, were not helpful for many reasons. First, calling authority and documentation often risked further alienating the teacher in question— leaving one to be perceived as a tattletale or someone not to be trusted. Others felt that these strategies were "too cruel" and would further damage an antagonist who was also vulnerable in the system (e.g., Sonia's paraprofessional/assistant teacher might lose a job she clearly needed). Thus, critical performance exercises elicited the multifaceted "rainbow" of interests, stances, powers, and vulnerabilities of their antagonists when trying out new solutions.

To keep records of a misbehaving child; to report trouble to the authorities—these courses of action were frequently performed. However, the real-time Theater of the Oppressed process and dialogue allowed spect-actors to reflect on and often reject these strategies as frequently "unreal" and/or unsatisfying. In contrast to other agentive strategies suggested, calls to authority and documentation seemed to diminish one's potential for action by deferring power to another source. Reporting to an authority figure such as an administrator or more senior colleague was often deemed to cause the protagonist teacher more trouble, alienation, and/or anxiety.

NETWORKS OF SUPPORT TO ENDURE STRUGGLE

Participants often referred to creating *networks of support* as a preferred alternative to keeping records or calling a superior. Preference was given to alliances with peer-teachers at the school site or with outside support groups to help endure the situation at hand. Rather than changing the behavior of the antagonist, spect-actors often suggested ways of tolerating an undisciplined student, an unprofessional colleague, or a cruel administrator until the situation's inevitable end. Marlena presented the unusual struggle of working as a paraprofessional with a lead teacher who was psychologically unstable, prone to unpredictable, and at times deceitful, behavior. We re-enacted a devastating moment when Marlena discovered the lead teacher had purposely denied misplacing or perhaps even stealing a child's "picture money." Marlena declined every solution proposed, explaining her only strategy was to endure the situation until she could receive her credential and would no longer have to work in that context. Here, too, Marlena recognized that the lead teacher was not just a "bad person" but had medically diagnosed mental health issues.

> MARLENA: I'm telling you she's on very strong medication, and she's being treated for depression. I think to myself, "Why start a war?" Right now, I'm at a point where I've got two more classes and I'm done.
>
> JOKER: And you're out of there. Once you're certified, you'll be out of that situation?
>
> MARLENA: Why start a war? I know she'll never change. She is an old mean lady, and she will never change. That's all.

The strategy to endure rather than fight for change at first seemed debilitating and relatively unsuccessful to us as "difficultators" trying to encourage more agentive solutions. However, the power of this work was made apparent the following week, when one of Marlena's teacher educators (Cahnmann-Taylor, the Joker in the dialogue above) visited her school. When Cahnmann-Taylor quietly asked her in the hallway outside the lead teacher's classroom how she was doing, Marlena replied with a wide grin, "Things are still as bad as they can be, but now I'm laughing!" Remembering the comic parodies that the Teachers Act Up! group enacted when performing her case, she said this network of critical performative friends had helped decrease her stress level and release the tension she experienced at her school site.

(IN)SUBORDINATION THROUGH PARODY AND HUMOR

One of the most striking elements of critical performative multicultural teacher education, as illuminated by Marlena's reflections with her lead teacher, was the elicitation of laughter. Regardless of whether suggested strategies were deemed "real" or not, we've found that the process of re-enactment itself promoted solidarity-building and was preparatory and agentive. Throughout recordings and transcripts of Teachers Acting Up! between 2003 and 2009, we saw frequent bursts of laughter expressed during group rehearsals. The laughter was most noticeable when two strategies were suggested: *strategic subordination* and *explicit insubordination*. In strategic subordination, participants pretended to play along with their antagonists, whereas when they *performed* insubordination, teachers acted in the rebellious ways they wished they could do (or say), but in reality could not. In both situations, teachers exaggerated their performances, and our workshops were filled with laughter and the sensation of play. Yolanda's case illustrates the use of these two strategies.

Strategic Subordination

In the initial three scenes of her story, a lead teacher, Yolanda, performed her frustration working with an administrator who she felt unfairly discriminated against her Spanish-accented pronunciation of English. The administrator repeatedly claimed to "not understand" what Yolanda was saying to her while in front of the students, causing Yolanda to feel devalued and out of control in her work environment.

In the re-enactment (or "take two") that follows, Yolanda played her antagonist principal, and another spect-actor, Ana, played the role of Yolanda, the thick-accented teacher. In this scene, the administrator didn't understand why no lesson plans had been prepared for Wednesday. The teacher repeatedly explained that her class was going on a field trip. Ana employed strategic subordination, exaggerating the character of an overly apologetic, incomprehensible, junior-ranked foreigner.

Bell rings. The principal abruptly comes into the teacher's classroom, waving a sheet of paper in the air.

PRINCIPAL [played by Yolanda]: I have one question about your lesson plan . . . What happened here on Wednesday, there's no . . . (*pointing at the page in her left hand*)

YOLANDA [played by Ana]: Ah, we have a (*with exaggerated mispronunciation*) "figh-trip."

PRINCIPAL: A what?

YOLANDA: A "figh-trip."

PRINCIPAL: A file trip?

YOLANDA: You understand me? (*pauses waiting for response*) No?

PRINCIPAL: (*emphasizing her words*) A FIIII-LE trip? What is a "file trip"?

YOLANDA: A "file-trip" (*stated matter-of-factly; looks at the principal to check for comprehension*) You can read right here (*pointing to the page*) "file-trip."

PRINCIPAL: Oh, a FIELD trip!

YOLANDA: Ohhh! A FIELD trip, 'scuse me, ay, you know (*spoken very quickly with a heavy accent*) sometimes you try to pronounce very well, exactly the words, but sometimes you miss, you know. When you teach Spanish . . .

PRINCIPAL: (*showing complete confusion*) Wha, wha, wha, what?
(*Hearty laughter from participating spect-actors.*)
JOKER: I want to hear from the people who were laughing. Why is
it so funny, what is it that's happening?
MARISOL: She's letting the principal know that, look, I *know* I have
an accent and I *know* that sometimes it's difficult for people to
understand me, but let's try.

Explicit Insubordination

In contrast to exaggerating the role of the bumbling "foreigner," as Ana
performed in the first intervention in Yolanda's case, another strategy that
elicited bursts of laughter was the portrayal of the explicitly insubordinate
underling. The protagonist was therefore giving the message that she was
not going to play along (as in the previous case in which strategic subordination was employed).

As we watched many generative stories being spect-acted, we noticed
that consistently, explicit insubordination was not perceived to be a "real"
option in the work world. Nevertheless, this strategy yielded important
solidarity building through the open expression of the otherwise dangerous, taboo, and unspeakable. The trans/script below was another take on
Yolanda's case, only this time the protagonist, played by Sara, was performed with defiance bordering on insolence. She performed an action
that other spect-actors wished they could perform, but were afraid of the
real-life consequences of such an act. In this context, however, explicitly
insubordinating served as a way to collectively imagine what they felt like
doing when confronted by such oppressive situations.

Bell rings. The principal enters Yolanda's room and interrupts her
as she is teaching.

PRINCIPAL [played by Yolanda]: Excuse me, I have a question about
your lesson plan for Wednesday. (*Pauses and looks blankly at
"Yolanda."*) A lesson plan?
YOLANDA [played by Sara]: (*Gasps and grabs the paper from the
principal's hands.*) I need to write we're going on a FIEEEELD
trip! (extremely *exaggerated pronunciation of "field trip," followed
by group laughter*)
PRINCIPAL: You're going where?
YOLANDA: On a field trip. (*writing on the paper in her hands*) We're
going to be at the Atlanta History Center. (*Passes the paper back
to the principal.*)

PRINCIPAL: The Atlanta History Center?
YOLANDA: Yes, all of third grade is going, including our class.
PRINCIPAL: You're what? (*looking quizzically at the paper in her hands*)
YOLANDA: All of third grade is going on the field trip.
PRINCIPAL: Where?
YOLANDA: See, I wrote it down, now *open* your eyes and *look*!
(*shouting, pointing to the paper in the administrator's hands,
followed by uproarious laughter from the rest of the group*)

In the "real world" of public schools, teachers do not openly argue
with or shame disrespectful colleagues—especially not their supervisors.
Yet in the context of Teachers Act Up!, these types of performances ("Now
open your eyes and *look*!") were not only acceptable but encouraged by
the Joker and other spect-actors. Teachers were not encouraged to com-
mit such acts against their antagonists, but to release the tension collectively through rehearsing possible and impossible reactions to a given
situation. In doing so, they went about generating strategies that pushed
against the boundaries of what was acceptable. These strategies encouraged the group of spect-actors to entertain the formerly unimagined and
perceived impossible—perhaps the only route to personal and social
change.

EVALUATING TEACHERS ACT UP!

Overall, there were clear, common understandings on a variety of issues
related to Acting Up! their professional lives presented by participating teachers in follow-up interviews. We presented still photos from our video shoots
to refresh participants' memories and asked them to reflect on their experiences with our Theatre of the Oppressed workshops; by and large, they saw
great benefits to participating, as well as pointing out some challenges to
Acting Up! Even those who did not like to stand up and act acknowledged
the benefits of problem-posing and problem solving performatively, taking into account interactional aspects that are commonly absent from
strictly verbal classroom interactions.

Positive Outcomes

- Participating teachers consistently reported, as one of the strengths,
  that there were no canned solutions offered in response to their issues. By bringing their issues to the group, many solutions were

collectively negotiated, and contextual specificities and personal preferences were respected and honored. According to one participant:

> People reacted differently to the same situation. That was fun to watch. I was the only one who knew the assistant teacher (the antagonist) and how she might react, but seeing different reactions gave me different perspectives to consider. It was actually empowering for me to see different options because sometimes I can only see one way to react and just ask, "Why, why, why?" Now I understand that I can open up and widen my view. If I see things differently, say things differently, and, you know, act differently, showing different body language, she *might*, you know, show a different side of her, too. So, human beings respond differently to different actions, so . . . Yeah, it was an empowering experience and I found great support. I think that's what I needed.

- Teachers came to recognize that they needed to embrace the dynamic nature of oppressor and oppressed roles. From different perspectives and across contexts, an individual might embody both roles. For example, after spect-actors performed Yolanda's case about the principal who claimed not to understand her accent, Marisol empathized with the challenges of being a monolingual American and turned her sympathies toward the plight of this demographic group:

> When they [Americans] don't understand a foreign accent, I don't think it's because they're evil. I honestly think people who have lived monolingual, monocultural lives in the United States are at a disadvantage understanding difference. We [bilingual people] are used to hearing it and they're not because they haven't been exposed. They're not as lucky as we are!

- Although some of the teachers saw humor as not being a real solution (as illustrated by the earlier example of Yolanda), they did see humor as a great resource for releasing stress and establishing the issue being discussed as a collective experience. Kim, one of the teachers, stated: "I might not agree with everything, but, it was, there's a comical touch, too, that helped me *relax* about the real situation." This reflects the feelings of a lot of teachers. As teacher educators, we noticed that when things got tense and protagonists rejected solutions, humor was used as a bonding strategy as well as a way to release tension. Marlena stated that although her situation had not been resolved, since she had to endure it for only a short amount of time, she could rely on the rehearsal of the ridiculous to help her cope, to laugh, privately and/or among peers.

- Teachers consistently found that although they initially felt uncomfortable, acting was more powerful than talking. They recognized again and again that words can yield multiple interpretations and acting one's situation or feeling gives a clearer perspective on the enacted situation. This is imperative, especially if those problematizing the situation are not directly familiar with the context of which the protagonist is part. According to Marlena:

  Sometimes words do not work. I like performing and it just helps me to really relive everything not only by words but by the movements. If I say I'm sad or I'm angry, you don't really know how angry I am. If I do the movement like that (looking at video footage of her performed case), I was actually on the floor, on the bottom. . . . And then you can really see how I feel if I let it go. It helps when you are performing for someone and there are people watching you. Although some people are shy, they don't want to perform. It probably depends on personality.

- One of the most frequent comments of participating teachers was that they saw direct links between performance and practice. Yolanda explained how she used one of the strategies suggested performatively—writing her words as she spoke—to navigate her challenges with a difficult principal. Others articulated taking one potential solution and applying it to their specific situations, truly using the Acting Up! forums as rehearsals for revolutions, even if small ones. Referring to her conflict with her teaching assistant, Sonia voiced:

  A theatre workshop is wonderful because you *have* support. There are lots and lots of options that you can think of—some are realistic, some are not. But, you know, they give *you* a *lot* of *strategies* that, "Oh! This might work. That might work." . . . Yeah, it, it was a powerful experience.

Specifically, Sonia took one spect-actor's suggestion to be mindful of her body language, particularly in moments of confrontation. She no longer slouches or cowers in the presence of her para-professional and consciously attempts to speak authoritatively in order to achieve a more equal flow of power. This change, however, was not immediate. Sonia explained:

> I feel like the Teachers Act Up! experience empowered me but I didn't realize it at the time. It was a little step that really helped resolve the problem later on. I learned that body language tells a lot when you're interacting with other people. You feel better and gradually you solve the problem or at least release the intensity of the conflict. You see the happy result if you really work at this.

- The theatre games and Image Theatre exercises, as explained in Chapters 3 and 4, served somewhat different purposes than did the Forum and Rainbow exercises described in Chapters 5 and 6. Although some teachers preferred games and Image Theatre exercises, others preferred to "difficultate" their own and their peers' stories. Some, like Carolina, argued for both, suggesting that the games can serve as a foundation for

> talking about specific things that bother the teachers, that they don't feel like they can voice, you know, their opinions, or that they can't go to the principal and say something. In this way, games could be beneficial in any work place to rethink relationships without having to get into specific details. Other times, games can warm people up to talking about their problems openly.

- Over and over, participants recognized the paramount relevance of generative themes. Because the cases and stories Acted Up! were relevant to many of the participating teachers, many of them found Forum Theater to be memorable and engaged in the internalization of strategies. One of the teachers said:

> We acted out what was happening and how those are *still* [recurring] moments and after that we would discuss *how* we deal with it. I remember that *before* we would act out the situation and later we would look into the possibilities, how to *deal* with the problems and *what would help me* to deal with the situation better. So, that opened up a lot of opportunities for me to *think* about the situation and for reflecting afterwards. It

really gave me insights that, "Oh, I did that? I did that? Oh! I should have done the *other* way." So it was really helpful.

- Many of the teachers with whom we worked over the years identified common experiences or experiences involving what Yolanda referred to as "the culture element." Many of the oppressive experiences teachers encountered had to do with cultural mismatches. Participating teachers shared a sense of the collective nature of the events. Often, several teachers could identify with oppressions that they initially thought were isolated instances and particular to their specific situation. They came to see that some of the oppressions they were experiencing were social (e.g., socioculturally and historically constructed) in nature and not personal. Together, they developed a supportive, trustworthy community in which they found support.

Obstacles to Overcome

According to teachers, Acting Up! can be a powerful tool for transforming classroom teaching, administrator-teacher relations, and the way teachers are educated in pre-service and in-service realms. Nevertheless, even after teachers articulated such possibilities, when asked if they could embrace this pedagogy in their classrooms, they clearly stated that tests drive many of their pedagogical choices. Furthermore, the amount of paperwork suppresses transformative possibilities in the classroom. Yolanda believed, "My main challenge is the paperwork . . . because every year it's more and more paperwork, more and more paperwork and more testing we have to do. And we don't have the support."

Obviously, it would be overly simplistic and disingenuous to ignore the challenges presented by teachers in their interviews regarding this kind of work. The major obstacles included adults' boundaries and discomfort with showing their feelings, as Marlena explained:

Adults have boundaries . . . some people I can see their faces if I presented this idea to them because I know some of them are shy and some of them would probably close the door in front of me. For that reason, no . . . because you're dealing with adults. They don't want to openly say what they feel, it's private, you're talking about your privacy—it's a private matter, you know a private thing, and you don't talk about it unless you're the type of person who wants to share your problems with everyone. I'm *not*, and I can see some people who are the same who don't want to present, you know, their real feelings, their real problems, to some other folks. In our group we have trust, we have a community. It's different.

Here, Marlena clearly conveyed the challenge of getting people to open up. We found that if people don't open up and convey their real, recursive oppressions, the techniques presented here are likely not going to result in transformation. So, it is important to be aware that when engaging in Acting Up!, some adults may not want to show their feelings, their vulnerabilities, unless they are part of a safe community. Fostering such a community is essential.

For example, another teacher, Carolina, conveyed that sometimes she didn't feel comfortable "being the center of attention." Although she recognized feeling empowered by Acting Up!, she related that she was "never very eager about the performing part." Further, she highlighted her uncertainty about a process where "her story" about challenges with a disruptive student lost specificity when it became "everyone's story":

> If I have a *specific* problem, I wanna sit down with one person, two people, the people that are directly, closely associated with this and just *talk* about it. I think because I and my school, we're expecting certain things, and so, if I have a situation, I *want* to talk to someone about it and come up with solutions just like *one on one more* than a large group.

Although we acknowledge Carolina's hesitation and discomfort, we embrace her response as a possible step in recognizing and naming the issues at stake as well as in recognizing the possibilities and limitations of this work. It is ultimately the Joker who is responsible for negotiating the ongoing tension between shaping scenes based on an individual's struggle (with a student, a paraprofessional, a colleague, and so on), while facilitating or difficultating scenes that are general enough so the content is pertinent to the group as a whole. The Joker is also ultimately responsible for generating participation and a group sense of comfort with the condition of discomfort, especially for participants who are shy or unfamiliar with theatre games or performance. The Joker mediates the risks involved in improvisational approaches to teacher education, filled as they are with the unpredictable and potentially taboo.

We have found that for people such as Carolina, working in smaller groups is the most productive. Sonia commented on differences in group size:

> I like what I *had* in the beginning. Because it was a smaller group, and we paid close attention to each individual's problems, we really went *deeply* into the problem-posing and problem-solving activities and discussions. But now our group's bigger, and I think it's more general now than pinpointing out one problem and just

really focusing on that. I may have benefited more from the real personal experience we had in smaller groups. But I think having larger groups is doing the right thing because, you know, time and resources are limited, and there're a *lot* more people needing help.

Nevertheless, when asked what she preferred, Sonia said: "I like it both ways because I can learn from *more* people's experiences. And I can take that to my own experience and I can analyze it a lot better here." So, it appears that smaller and larger groups both have advantages in Acting Up! for change.

Despite its obstacles and shortcomings, as articulated earlier by participating teachers, Acting Up! had a direct and positive effect on most teachers' practices, as indicated by survey results. For example, in a post–focus group interview, Marisol commented on her agentive communication strategies:

> Because before, I used to talk shit, let's say. You know I would get mad [about a teacher ignoring ESOL students] and just complain after work to my friends. And now, I try to be more direct with the person, "Yeah, sometimes ESOL students don't understand," I tell them. Then I say, "It happens, and this is why." I'll say, "Let's try to understand and through understanding we can work with it."

Such comments indicate that performative techniques helped teachers tap into their own voices of authority and explanatory power, rethinking power relations that they initially perceived as oppressive. But did change actually take place? What tangible effect has this work had on participants in interactions with students, colleagues, parents, administrators, and professors?

The critical pedagogue-idealist may hope that participants experience explosive, epiphanic moments, similar to the experience of the Brazilian peasant who approached Boal to take up arms against the government (as noted in Chapter 2). However, in recent discussions of Boalian work, Carmen Medina (2007) reminded us that the effects of educative work, regardless of theoretical framework, are rarely visible in immediate, concrete ways. We came to acknowledge that evidence of change must occur over periods of time that extend well beyond the length of any program, workshop, or study. So, what we present in this book are the inklings of larger transformative actions, at both the personal and the societal level. Participants said explicitly that some of the strategies spect-actors enacted were viable enough to try when conflict arose.

Other instrumental responses that we observed over time have been the creation of networks among Teachers Act Up! participants as well as between Teachers Act Up! participants and other school-based professionals enduring and surviving through antagonisms, a choice made easier through networks of support and the parody and humor generated together. However, we acknowledge that, at times, participants found it necessary to leave a caustic site and seek employment at another school, pursue higher degrees, and/or seek positions of increasing power and authority (e.g., becoming instructional coaches or administrators).

POSSIBILITIES AND CHALLENGES: THEATRE OF THE OPPRESSED IN TEACHER EDUCATION

Teachers Act Up! merges practices and theories from multicultural education, critical pedagogy, and performance. In so doing, we believe that our approach contributes to the quality of teacher education as it addresses realistic, stressful, potentially oppressive situations and relationships in multicultural classrooms and schools. Our goals are to enhance teachers' sense of themselves as capable and vital agents for change, thereby improving teacher practice and teacher retention. We hope that these theatre activities provide fresh ideas for developing critical, embodied approaches to curriculum.

Findings from our studies of performance practices in teacher education indicate that there are many and varied advantages to such practices, tapping into aspects of learning along a continuum from thinking to feeling. We believe that changing the dynamics of teacher education from top-down, text-based monologic methods to those that encourage cooperative, life-based dialogues between teacher-educators and pre- or in-service teachers will allow teachers to learn methodologies to be employed in their own settings and to experiment with teaching, consequently pushing the limits of what's possible in the critical multicultural classroom.

Starting literally with the text of teachers' lives as resources for embodied learning makes multicultural education immediately relevant to all participants (Burgoyne et al., 2005; Collins, 2000; Kaye & Ragusa, 1998; Nieto, 1999; Pineau, 2002) and puts critical pedagogy into practice. We do not eschew text-based learning in teacher education, nor do we disregard the utility of traditional texts to study and document learning. However, we believe that critical, embodied, and performative practices have long been missing in teacher education. Teachers Act Up! has demonstrated unexpected enthusiasm and reflective learning in ways we have not observed or practiced in traditional, multicultural teacher education courses that, despite critical intentions, are largely stationary, inactive, and theory driven.

Leaving the safe syllabus and methodologies of "the known" to experiment with generative themes representing teachers' everyday experiences and realities poses a greater risk for teacher educators who are positioned to face and facilitate the unpredictable and the unknown. It is a risky yet worthy journey, as we have seen our performative work influence K–12 classrooms. When we are asking teachers to be vulnerable and share their struggles with us, it is only fair that we place ourselves in a vulnerable position as we facilitate the Teachers Act Up! workshops. By doing so, we are truly able to engage in dialectical authority (Freire, 1970, 1985; Giroux, 1997; Horton & Freire, 1990; Kincheloe, 2005; Kincheloe & Steinberg, 1998; McLaren, 2000).

As teacher educators, we do not have absolute answers to teachers' real, day-to-day concerns—e.g., how to work with an uncooperative, unstable, or unsafe colleague; how to manage students who are disengaged, disrespectful, or even, at times, violent, in the classroom. Nevertheless, through Teachers Act Up!, we learned that not having the answers is a strength, allowing teachers' collective wisdom to come forth and unforeseen challenges to become known. Through Theatre of the Oppressed, we learned to demechanize our bodies (see Chapter 3 for more on this), reach outside routine behaviors, and re-imagine possibilities—real, unreal, and surreal—to parody, play, and transform lived experience.

We are aware that this kind of work presents risks, as well as possibilities for change, in teacher education during times of testing pressures against liberatory practices. Within a context shaped by legislation such as No Child Left Behind (or, as many teachers jokingly say, "No Teacher Left Standing"), as well as district- and school-mandated testing and curriculum, many teachers and teacher educators feel constricted in both the content and form that education takes.

Nonetheless, we continue to pose questions regarding the process as we learn along the way. We invite you to ask yourself some of these very questions, acknowledging that there are multiple possibilities to respond to each of these problems posed:

- When subjects such as racism, linguistic discrimination, stereotyping, and other edgy material become the central focus, how do educators and teacher educators respond?
- What training and trust are required to touch upon sensitive and often silenced material with the dignity and articulation that such issues deserve?

• In a mandated testing culture, what are the consequences of taking class time to pose unanswerable questions?

Although we may have speculations and considerations, we do not pretend that these are simplistic issues that are easily resolved by finite solutions. We are aware of the risks taken as we approach volatile and seemingly forbidden issues, but risky teaching is necessary for transformative outcomes (Hermann-Wilmarth, 2003). In such a vein, we propose that using Theatre of the Oppressed has the potential to transform teacher education into much-needed critical multicultural teacher education.

Based on our experiences, we know that such a performative approach to teacher education pushes beyond the limits of what's known, acceptable, feasible, and practiced, as it asks teachers as spect-actors to explore options rather than solutions and to rehearse the impossible rather than the perceived inevitable. Though the situations and actors may change, sites of struggle are present and recurrent in teachers' lives. New approaches to critical multicultural teacher education are much needed. This is particularly true of approaches like this one, which raises awareness of the moving and omnipresent "multiplicity of force relations" (Foucault, 1978, pp. 92–93) that operate in teachers' lives.

Through Teachers Act Up!, we seek to acknowledge the complex and fluid task of teaching in a diverse world and rehearse transformative possibilities leading to more humane relations, more respect and appreciation of diversities, and the repositioning of teachers and learners, actors and spectators, objects and subjects. As we analyze data from the Teachers Act Up! project, we find evidence of the dynamic potential for blurring boundaries between teacher and learner, between oppressed and oppressor, between the art and science of teacher education. Performatively and collectively, we redefine authority as dialectical and focus on facilitation (or difficultation) of complex issues and problem-posing. Collectively, we can take risks, rehearse, and enact change.

Teatro as a Collective Problem-Solving Activity for Social Action: An Afterword

TEACHERS ACT UP! takes a fresh approach to "remediating" the culture of schooling for teachers of students from nondominant communities; here *remediating* refers to a system's reorganization in which new tools with new purposes are introduced to create anew functional systems with transformative potential for their participants (Gutiérrez, Morales, & Martinez, 2009). The premise advanced by authors Cahnmann-Taylor and Souto-Manning is that new forms of mediation are needed in order for teachers to envision a new teaching self, new ways to organize learning, and new practices to become "multiculturally competent." By helping teachers imagine "as if" they lived in an ideal pedagogical context in which the contradictions of schooling are made visible, teachers can begin to refashion themselves as agents, actors, and spect-actors who can engage in processes of change that have material effects on their lives and the lives of their students.

We learn through the Acting Up workshops that rehearsed dialogue situated in the everyday challenges teachers experience serves to "open up communication, to break down barriers, you know, cultural barriers" (p. 226), as one teacher, Yolanda, summed it up. Drawing on critical pedagogy, critical multiculturalism, and Theatre of the Oppressed (Boal, 1979), Acting Up becomes a designed environment where embodied learning is privileged and the imagination is used to seek alternative frames for the myriad complex problems encountered in the everyday lives of teachers and students. In this context, as in my own work, *Teatro del Oprimido* (Theatre of the Oppressed) serves as a new form of public problem solving in which participants "try out" new discourses, perspectives, and ways of mediating contradictions. One of the important goals of Cahnmann-Taylor and Souto-Manning's work is to help teachers see the contradictions in the activity system of U.S. schooling as the primary antagonists—contradictions that warrant what I term a new "pedagogical imagination" to instantiate a critical humanist pedagogy for both teachers and students.

But rather than viewing this intervention through the theoretical lenses employed in the text, I would like to call attention to the ways the

141

Acting Up workshop and the vehicle of *Teatro* serve as powerful mediating artifacts for the development of both social and cognitive change. *Teachers Act Up!* is an argument for teacher apprenticeship organized around a broader notion of teacher learning where the use of rich meditational means allow participants to collaborate in ways not afforded teachers-in-practice. Of significance, this apprenticeship process offered through the workshops requires collective problem-solving activity in which learning is local, reciprocal, and distributed and leads to new forms of learning and a reframing of the role of teacher in teaching/learning processes. By embodying the constraints that teachers face in the classroom and beyond, we witness teachers who begin to problem-solve together and to articulate and frame dilemmas in ways that can help make solutions more evident.

Teatro, grounded in Boal, is conceptualized as a dialectic between the individual and social, between the world as it is and the world as it could be, and attempts to address a problematic—one that is complicated by a joker, the "difficultator," whose role it is to add complexity to the ways we generally identify and describe problems. As we learn from *Teachers Act Up!*, participating in these new practices involves risk-taking, trust, and the ability to deal with ambiguity and discomfort, as we saw in Carolina's case. Here, the joker, like the hybrid mythical cyber wizard, El Maga in our own work (Gutiérrez, Baquedano-López, & Álvarez, 2001), must carefully negotiate the tensions that emerge as participants attempt to make meaning of what is being learned in the workshop, of the feelings experienced, and the new understandings that emerge in situ. It is the joker who can engage participants, incite enthusiasm and discomfort, and mediate the risks involved in making one's individual, as well as collective, problems transparent.

Drawing on sociocultural notions of play as a leading activity and the imaginary situation (Griffin & Cole, 1984; Vygotsky, 1978), *Teatro* is a form of "deep play" designed to promote collective problem-solving activity for the participants toward the development of a newly imagined future. Through the enactment of real and immediate educational and sociocultural situations, participants are required to observe with the intent of intervening in various scenarios in some form of problem-solving behavior, that is, to enact and discuss scenarios of the ideal world where current contradictions are resolved toward the ideal. In embodying the present and the future in Image theatre, participants have opportunities to reconceive of the past, and to see contradictions that constrain opportunities for transformation. Following Boal (1979), the process involves imaging/embodying the actual image (the world as it is), the ideal image (the world as it could be), and ultimately the transitional image (the transformation).

It is in this process that teachers can, in the Boalian sense, train themselves for real action.

However, it would be a mistake to see the imagination as the key ingredient in the teachers' transformation; instead, imagination is inextricably linked to a critical analysis of the historical, as well as to the here and now, to envisioning the "world as it could be." This critical analysis, however, cannot be developed solely through *Teatro* and its practices. I would expand the meditational tools that are a part of the Acting Up workshops to include social and learning theories that can help teachers understand and inhabit the transformative potential of Image theatre. Theory, like theatre, is a tool that can open up the ways we see the world, its contradictions, and its possibilities. We need to resist the tendency to dichotomize theory and practice and to experience the transformative potential of theory-in-practice. For me, *Teachers Act Up!* is theory-in-practice.

—Kris D. Gutiérrez

REFERENCES

Boal, A. (1979). *Theatre of the oppressed.* New York: Theatre Communications Group.

Griffin, P., & Cole, M. (1984). Current activity for the future: The zo-ped. In B. Rogoff & J. V. Wertsch (Eds.), *Children's learning in the "zone of proximal development": New directions for child development* (pp. 45–63). San Francisco: Jossey-Bass.

Gutiérrez, K., Baquedano-López, P., & Álvarez, H. (2001). Literacy as hybridity: Moving beyond bilingualism in urban classrooms. In M. de la Luz Reyes & J. Halcón (Eds.), *The best for our children: Critical perspectives on literacy for Latino students* (pp. 122–141). New York: Teachers College Press.

Gutiérrez, K., Morales, P. L., & Martinez, D. (2009). Re-mediating Literacy: Culture, difference, and learning for students from non-dominant communities. *Review of Research in Educational Research, 33,* 212–245.

Vygotsky, L. S. (1978). *Mind in society: The development of higher psychological processes* (M. Cole, V. John-Steiner, S. Scribner, & E. Souberman, Eds. & Trans.). Cambridge, MA: Harvard University Press. (Original work published 1934)

Reflecting on Embodied Teacher Education: A Teacher's Testimony

IN THE SPIRIT of dialogue and sharing the stage (or the page, if you will), we include a complete interview between a teacher educator and Yolanda (whom you met in the Conclusion), regarding her experiences with Theatre of the Oppressed workshops. Although we shared excerpts from other teachers' interviews in the Conclusion when reporting our research findings, we believe Yolanda's entire interview reveals so many of the powerful lessons we have learned from sharing Theatre of the Oppressed activities in our classrooms, workshops, and grant program activities.

To review, Yolanda's case concerned her struggles working with an American-born principal who repeatedly claimed not to understand Yolanda's Spanish-accented English. Yolanda not only frequently felt misunderstood, but also emotionally badgered in an environment she felt was hostile both to students and teachers for whom English was not their first language. The interview presented below, conducted by a doctoral student and one of our research team members, illuminates the many implications performance-based work can have on teacher education.

INTERVIEWER: What's your understanding of Theatre of the Oppressed?

YOLANDA: My understanding is that it's a channel to share what your experiences of oppression are, and for others to share, too. You experience what others are going through and you help give suggestions, solutions, and share those with others who feel oppressed, too.

INTERVIEWER: Can you tell us a little bit about what you remember from the session when we focused on your situation with your principal?

YOLANDA: I remember the different solutions that the participants had for my situation. . . . I remember that when I was listening to them give solutions I said to myself, "This is not going to work with *my* principal." (laughs) . . . It depends on the person you're dealing with. A lot of the solutions were too direct and in your face, you know, and she wouldn't have reacted very positively to that. But there were also good solutions, and it

made me think a lot about, you know, other ways I could have
addressed the situation.

INTERVIEWER: And what was your reaction to the other group
solutions?

YOLANDA: Ah, they were very funny to me, you know (laughs)?
Like I said, there were good solutions according to who you're
dealing with, the person you're dealing with, so I was amazed
at their brazenness, you know? I mean, I thought—"Do you
talk that way to your principal?" You know, I wasn't sure if
they would really do that.

INTERVIEWER: You told me that some of the solutions were funny
for you. What did they mean to you?

YOLANDA: (*laughter*) Ah, that it could turn into a funny situation,
but like I said it was not funny to me at the time, you know,
because it was a situation that I was dealing with every day
with a person of great authority. If I say something that may
be funny to me, it may not be funny to her, she could retali-
ate a little, work against me, and it would affect me in a
negative way, so, the lesson was good because I said, "You
know, I could turn this into something humorous, into
something light hearted and humorous, but not with my
principal" (*laughter*).

INTERVIEWER: What do you think was the purpose of these activities?

YOLANDA: To reflect; I think a lot of it is reflecting on, you know,
my situation, my experiences, and looking at others' perspectives, as to how, you know, you can solve these problems and
turn these bad experiences around into good experiences. So,
to me, it's a time for reflection, that's what I get out of these
activities.

INTERVIEWER: And what did you get?

YOLANDA: What did I get from that? Well, I realized that my
coworkers went through the same situation, I didn't know it. I
don't think people realize that with ESOL people, that principals do react like that.

INTERVIEWER: Okay. What do you think is of value in coming
together to perform teachers' experiences?

YOLANDA: It's good. I think the most valuable thing is to know that
other teachers may be going through the same thing that
you're going through, and that everyone has their own
personal struggles and there's a little bit of confidence in
knowing that "Well, I'm not the only one that's going through
this." So, at first, I thought maybe it's me, my personality or

my character, but no, it's that a lot of the struggles basically have to do with being from another culture. That's what I learned from the others, doing these activities.

INTERVIEWER: Do you think there are any differences between getting together to talk about struggles and solutions versus acting them out?

YOLANDA: Yes. I think acting them out you get more involved. If you just sit down and talk about it, it goes in one ear and goes out the other. But if you act it out, you know, it's like you've lived through that experience a couple of minutes, and I think that's why we practice acting it out, doing it rather than just listening or talking about it.

INTERVIEWER: Tell me about how you felt immediately after the acting of your case?

YOLANDA: I remember thinking, "Hum, well maybe it's not really that big of a deal." You know? I'm more calm. I'm more at peace on the job, and I'm more focused and I'm more resilient, and I feel as if it's helped me mature professionally also. I'm more professionally mature now.

INTERVIEWER: What did you do in your next interaction with the principal after the Theatre of the Oppressed?

YOLANDA: Oh, I remember the next interaction wasn't that difficult, you know, there were some times she couldn't understand or she claimed she didn't understand and she asked me to repeat but then I didn't respond as strongly as before. I took it more lightly, and it didn't bother me like it did before. After the workshop, I had some more solutions. Some said, just ignore it, or next time go in with it written, write it out. That's what I did. I wrote it and I pointed to what I'd written, so, as I was talking, I was pointing to what I'd written. I tried that, and it worked better for me.

INTERVIEWER: What are your thoughts on the process we've developed during the last focus groups?

YOLANDA: Well, planning, acting, suggestions, discussion is a format that we should use every day in teaching, too, you know? You plan what you're going to do, then you act, act out the lesson. Suggestions, you see what the results are from the children. Are they learning? Are they not learning? And then there are more suggestions and discussions. I think that format is what we should use professionally and personally in life. It's a good process for finding solutions or accomplishing things in life and in teaching.

INTERVIEWER: What is the most beneficial aspect of Theatre of the Oppressed for you?

YOLANDA: Being able to share my experience and being able to see others' experiences too. Basically, it unifies us more as teachers. You know, as a bilingual teacher or ESOL teacher, I think it forms a stronger bond between us.

INTERVIEWER: And what is the least beneficial?

YOLANDA: The least beneficial things to me were the funny solutions to serious problems. That was a big release, but they didn't help me because they weren't realistic.

INTERVIEWER: Okay. How useful is this method for educators?

YOLANDA: Very useful. As educators we need to reflect more, spend some more time on reflection, analyzing how we are doing as educators, as professionals, and as human beings. I think it's very useful. It's a good strategy to use. It is teaching strategies also to deal with our students. So, I think it's a good strategy you can implement in the classroom also.

INTERVIEWER: Okay, is there anything more that you'd want to share about these activities, of Theatre of the Oppressed, of focus groups in general?

YOLANDA: I really enjoy it. I enjoy Theatre of the Oppressed, I enjoy the focus groups very much. Because we don't have time in our schools, you know, we don't have time to come together and discuss these types of issues, which would be like opening up a panel. We don't do it in schools because nobody wants to address that. We need those, we need that part. We need that time to focus, to reflect.

INTERVIEWER: Do you think that this Theatre of the Oppressed could be used at the schools with administrators?

YOLANDA: Yeah. I think it would be a very, very, very good tool to facilitate communication between the administration and teachers, especially teachers from other countries. But I don't know if they would want to (*laughter*) because it's too in your face and I don't think they'd want that. I don't think they're ready for that . . . because the whole thing is political. They wouldn't want to discuss those types of issues because nobody wants to go there, you know? Everybody's acting like the issues don't exist. It is very much alive in their minds, but nobody wants to address them because in the end it opens up a whole can of worms. But it's needed [Theatre of the Oppressed] to open up communication, to break down barriers, you know, cultural barriers.

INTERVIEWER: Okay. I think these are all my questions. Do you have any questions that you would like to ask or something to share?

YOLANDA: The only thing I think is that when you're talking about colleges, in teacher preparation, they need to prepare teachers better for the cultural variety that they're going to see and experience in their students. I think these student teachers are coming out thinking they are going to teach the same type of child they were—the whole class is going to be made up of little Tommies or little Susies. And I think that the teacher education program needs to prepare them a little bit more for that diversity. Because it's overwhelming for them, not knowing, you know, "How do I help this child? What do I do? Why does this child act like this? Why does this child like to do this?" Because many teachers and administrators don't understand the worlds the children are coming from. They don't understand the many perspectives, the many ways of seeing a situation, the many solutions we explore in this work [Theatre of the Oppressed]. The teacher education programs need to prepare teachers to teach in all schools, to really understand cultures and diversity.

References

Abt-Perkins, D., & Gomez, M. L. (1993). A good place to begin: Examining our personal perspectives. *Language Arts, 70*(3), 193–204.

Allen, J. (2007). *Creating welcoming schools: A practical guide to home-school partnerships with diverse families.* New York; Newark, DE: Teachers College Press; International Reading Association.

Allen, J., & Hermann-Wilmarth, J. (2004). Cultural construction zones. *Journal of Teacher Education, 55*(3), 214–226.

Anderson, G. T. (2005). Innovations in early childhood teacher education: Reflections on practice. *Journal of Early Childhood Teacher Education, 26*(1), 91–95.

Ayers, W. (2004). *Teaching toward freedom: Moral commitment and ethical action in the classroom.* Boston: Beacon Press.

Bakhtin, M. (1984). *Rabelais and his world.* (Trans. H. Iswolsky). Bloomington, IN: Indiana University Press.

Ball, A., & Lardner, T. (2006). *African-American literacies unleashed: Vernacular English and the composition classroom.* Carbondale, IL: Southern Illinois University Press.

Ball, A. (2006). *Multicultural strategies for education and social change: Catheriners of the torch in the United States and South Africa.* New York: Teachers College Press.

Banks, J. (2007). Series foreword. In C. D. Lee (Ed.), *Culture, literacy, and learning* (pp. xi–xv). New York: Teachers College Press.

Banks, J. A. (1995). Multicultural education and curriculum transformation. *Journal of Negro Education, 64*(4), 390.

Barker, C. (1983/1977). *Theatre games: A new approach to drama training.* London; New York: Methuen London; Drama Book Publishers Distributor.

Bartolomé, L. I. (2002). Creating an equal playing field: Teachers as advocates, border crossers, and cultural brokers. In Z. F. Beykont (Ed.), *The power of culture: Teaching across language difference* (pp. 167–191). Cambridge, MA: Harvard Educational Publishing Group.

Boal, A. (1974). *Teatro del oprimido.* Buenos Aires, Argentina: Ediciones de la Flor.

Boal, A. (1979). *Theatre of the oppressed.* New York: Theatre Communications Group.

Boal, A. (1992). *Games for actors and non-actors.* London; New York: Routledge.

Boal, A. (1995). *Rainbow of desire: The Boal method of theatre and therapy politics* (A. Jackson, Trans.). London: Routledge.

Boal, A. (1998). *Legislative theatre: Using performance to make politics.* London; New York: Routledge.

Boal, A. (2001). Force for change: To "act" is to perform and to take action for social change. *Resurgence, 204*. Retrieved May 7, 2009, from http://www. resurgence.org/magazine/issue204.html

Boal, A. (2002). *Games for actors and non-actors* (2nd ed.). London; New York: Routledge.

Boal, A. (2005). *Democracy now: The war and peace report*. Retrieved May 3, 2009, from http://www.democracynow.org/2005/6/3/famed_brazilian_artist_augusto_boal_on

Brecht Forum. (2009, May 2). *Rainbow of desire into Forum theatre*. Retrieved May 2, 2009, from http://brechtforum.org/boal2–2009

Brown, K. H., & Gillespie, D. (1997). "We become brave by doing brave acts": Teaching moral courage through the theatre of the oppressed. *Literature and Medicine, 16* (1), 108–120.

Burgoyne, S., Welch, S., Cockrell, K., Neville, H., Placier, P., & Davidson, M., Share, T., & Fisher, B. (2005). *Researching Theatre of the Oppressed: A scholarship of teaching and learning project*. Retrieved November 15, 2006, from http://facctr.wcu.edu/mountainrise/archive/vol2no1/html/researching_theatre.html

Cahnmann, M. (2001). *Shifting metaphors: Of war and reimagination in the bilingual classroom*. Unpublished doctoral dissertation, University of Pennsylvania, Philadelphia.

Cahnmann, M. (2006). Reading, living, and writing bilingual poetry as scholARTistry in the language arts classroom. *Language Arts, 83*(4), 341–351.

Cahnmann, M., Rymes, B., & Souto-Manning, M. (2005). Using critical discourse analysis to understand and facilitate identification processes of bilingual adults becoming teachers. *Critical Inquiry in Language Studies: An International Journal, 2* (4), 195–213.

Cahnmann-Taylor, M., & Siegesmund, R. (Eds.). (2008). *Arts-based inquiry in diverse learning communities: Foundations for practice*. New York: Taylor & Francis.

Cahnmann-Taylor, M., Wooten, J., Souto-Manning, M., & Dice, J. (2009). The art & science of educational inquiry: Analysis of performance-based focus groups with novice bilingual teachers. *Teachers College Record, 11*(11), 2535–2559.

Campbell, A. M. (1995). Questions from Rio + representatives of the offshore-island group from Britain attend the international festival of the theatre-of-the-oppressed in Rio-de-Janeiro. *Contemporary Theatre Review, 3*, 109–119.

Carter, R., & Goodwin, A. L. (1994). Racial identity and education. *Review of Research in Education, 20*, 291–336.

Cixous, H. (1993). *Three steps on the ladder of writing*. New York: Columbia University Press.

Cochran-Smith, M., & Fries, M. K. (2001). Sticks, stones, and ideology: The discourse of reform in teacher education. *Educational Researcher, 30*(8), 3–15.

Cochran-Smith, M., & Lytle, S. L. (1990). Research on teaching and teacher research: The issues that divide. *Educational Researcher, 19*, 2–11.

Collins, P. H. (2000). *Black feminist thought: Knowledge, consciousness, and the politics of empowerment* (2nd ed.). New York: Routledge.

Connelly, F. M., & Clandinin, D. J. (1988). *Teachers as curriculum planners: Narratives of experience*. New York: Teachers College Press.

Cowhey, M. (2006). *Black ants and Buddhists: Thinking critically and teaching differently in the primary grades.* Portland, ME: Stenhouse Publishers.

Crawford, J. (2004). *Educating English learners: Language diversity in the classroom.* Los Angeles: Bilingual Educational Services, Inc.

Creel, G., Kuhne, M., & Riggle, M. (2000). See the Boal, be the Boal: Theatre of the oppressed and composition courses. *Teaching English in the Two-Year College, 28*(2), 141–156.

Darling-Hammond, L. (2000). How teacher education matters. *Journal of Teacher Education, 51,* 166–173.

Darling-Hammond, L. (2007a). Foreword. In C. D. Lee, *Culture, literacy, and learning: Taking bloom in the midst of the whirlwind* (pp. xvii–xxii). New York: Teachers College Press.

Darling-Hammond, L. (2007b). Race, inequality and educational accountability: The irony of "No Child Left Behind". *Race Ethnicity and Education, 10,* 245–260.

Darling-Hammond, L. (2008). The case for university-based teacher education. In M. Cochran-Smith, S. Feinan-Nemser, & D. J. McIntyre (Eds.), *Handbook of research on teacher education: Enduring questions in changing contexts* (pp. 333–346). New York; London, UK: Routledge.

Delpit, L. (1988). The silenced dialogue: Power and pedagogy in educating other people's children. *Harvard Educational Review, 58*(3), 280–298.

Dyson, A. H., & Genishi, C. (2005). *On the case: Approaches to language and literacy research.* New York: Teachers College Press.

Edelsky, C. (1981). Who's got the floor? *Language in Society, 10,* 383–421.

Edmond, G., & Tilley, E. (2007, October 16). Beyond role play: Workplace theatre and employee relations. Retrieved October 16, 2007, from http://praxis.massey.ac.nz/fileadmin/praxis/papers/GEdmondETilleyPaper_20.pdf

Eisner, E. (1991). *The enlightened eye: Qualitative inquiry and the enhancement of educational practice.* New York: Macmillan.

Eisner, E. (2002). *The arts and the creation of mind.* New Haven, CT: Yale University Press.

Estrella, O., Vossoughi, S., & Espinoza, M. (2006, April). Teatro, play & imagination: The creative engagement of social life. Paper presented at the American Educational Research Association Conference, San Francisco, CA.

Fennimore, B. S. (2000). *Talk matters: Refocusing the language of public schooling.* New York: Teachers College Press.

Ferrand, L. (1995). Forum theater with carers: The use of forum theater in specific community settings. *Contemporary Theatre Review, 3,* 23–37.

Foucault, M. (1977). *Discipline and punish.* London, UK: Allen Lane.

Foucault, M. (1978). *The history of sexuality: An introduction.* New York: Vintage Books.

Foucault, M. (2001). *The essential work 3: Power.* Harmondsworth, UK: Penguin.

Freire, P. (1970). *Pedagogy of the oppressed.* New York: Continuum.

Freire, P. (1985). *The politics of education.* Westport, CT: Bergin & Garvin.

Freire P. (1998a) *Pedagogy of freedom: Ethics, democracy, and civic courage.* Lanham, MD: Rowman & Littlefield.

Freire, P. (1998b). *Teachers as cultural workers: Letters to those who dare teach.* Oxford: Westview.

Geertz, C. (1973). *The interpretation of cultures: Selected essays.* New York: Basic Books.

Genishi, C., & Goodwin, A. L. (Eds.). (2008). *Diversities in early childhood education: Rethinking and doing.* New York: Routledge.

Giroux, H. (1997). *Pedagogy and the politics of hope: Theory, culture, and schooling.* Boulder, CO: Westview.

Goffman, E. (1959). *The presentation of self in everyday life.* Garden City, NY: Doubleday.

Gomez, M. L. (1992). Breaking silences: Building new stories of classroom life through teacher transformation. In S. Kessler & B. B. Swadener (Eds.), *Reconceptualizing the early childhood curriculum: Beginning the dialogue* (pp. 165–188). New York: Teachers College Press.

Gomez, M. L. (2002). The role of talk in learning to teach. *Curriculum and Teaching, 17*(2), 37.

Gomez, M. L., & Abt-Perkins, D. (1995). Sharing stories for practice, analysis, and critique. *Education Research and Perspectives, 22*(1), 39–52.

Gomez, M. L., & Tabachnick, B. R. (1992). Telling teaching stories. *Teaching Education, 4*(2), 129–138.

Goodwin, A. L., Cheruvu, R., & Genishi, C. (2008). Responding to multiple diversities in early childhood education: How far have we come? In C. Genishi & A. L Goodwin (Eds.), *Diversities in early childhood: Rethinking and doing* (pp. 3–10). New York: Routledge.

Grant, C. A., & Sleeter, C. E. (1996). *After the school bell rings.* London, UK; Washington, DC: Falmer Press.

Gutiérrez, K. (2008). Developing a sociocritical literacy in the third space. *Reading Research Quarterly, 43*(2), 148–164.

Harman, R., & French, K. (2004). Critical performance pedagogy: A feasible praxis for teacher education. In J. O'Donnell, M. Pruyn, & R. C. Chavez (Eds.), *Social justice in these times* (pp. 97–115). Information Age Publishing.

Harste, J., Lewison, M., Leland, C., Ociepka, A., & Vasquez, V. (2000). Exploring critical literacy: You can hear a pin drop. In B. Graham (Ed.), *Trends and issues in elementary language arts* (pp. 203–218). Urbana, IL: NCTE.

Heathcote, D., & Bolton, G. M. (1995). *Drama for learning: Dorothy Heathcote's mantle of the expert approach to education.* Portmouth, NH: Heinemann.

Hermann-Wilmarth, J. (2003). Risky teaching. In B. Shockley-Bisplinghoff, J. Olson, & M. Commeyras (Eds.), *Teachers as readers: Perspectives on the importance of reading in teachers' classrooms and lives* (pp. 110–119). Newark, DE: International Reading Association.

Hirsch, E. (1999). *How to read a poem and fall in love with poetry.* New York: Harcourt.

Hoffman, D. M. (1996). Culture and self in multicultural education: Reflections on discourse, text, and practice. *American Educational Research Journal, 33*(3), 545–569.

hooks, b. (1994). *Teaching to transgress: Education as the practice of freedom.* New York: Routledge.

Horton, M., & Freire, P. (1990). *We make the road by walking: Conversations on education and social change.* Philadelphia: Temple University Press.

Howard, G. R. (2006). *We can't teach what we don't know: White teachers, multiracial schools*. New York: Teachers College Press.

Houston, S., Magill, T., McCollum, M., & Spratt, T. (2001). Developing creative solutions to the problems of children and their families: Communicative reason and the use of Forum Theatre. *Child & Family Social Work, 6*, 285–293.

Hughes, E. (1999). If you have sun and you have rain you get a rainbow: Creating meaningful curriculum. *Journal of Early Childhood Teacher Education, 20*, 89–100.

Jackson, A. (1995). Translator's introduction. *Rainbow of desire: The Boal method of theatre and therapy politics* (pp. xviii–xxvi). London; New York: Routledge.

Jensen, M. (1999). Developing pedagogical knowledge through teacher-written case stories. *Journal of Early Childhood Teacher Education, 20*, 181–184.

Kaye, C., & Ragusa, G. (1998). *Boal's mirror: Reflections for teacher education*. ERIC Document Reproduction Service No. ED 419787.

Kincheloe, J. L. (2005). *Critical pedagogy*. New York: Peter Lang.

Kincheloe, J. L. (2008). *Knowledge and critical pedagogy: An introduction*. Dordrecht: Springer.

Kincheloe, J., & Steinberg, S. (1998). Lesson plans from the outer limits: Unauthorized methods. In J. Kincheloe & S. Steinberg (Eds.), *Unauthorized methods: Strategies for critical teaching* (pp. 1–23). New York: Routledge.

Kozol, J. (2007). *Letters to a young teacher*. New York: Crown.

Larson, J., & Marsh, J. (2005). *Making literacy real: Theories and practices for learning and teaching*. Thousand Oaks, CA: Sage.

Lee, C. D. (2007). *Culture, literacy, and learning: Taking bloom in the midst of the whirlwind*. New York: Teachers College Press.

Lesko, N. (2001). *Act your age!: A cultural construction of adolescence*. New York: Routledge.

Lobman, C., & Lundquist, M. (2007). *Unscripted learning: Using improv activities across the K–8 curriculum*. New York: Teachers College Press.

Logan, C. R., DiCintio, M., Cox, K. E., & Turner, J. C. (1995, October). *The relationship between teacher perceptions and observations of motivational practices in the classroom*. Paper presented at the Annual Meeting of the Northeastern Educational Research Association. Ellenville, NY.

Long, S., Anderson, C., Clark, M., & McCraw, B. (2008). Going beyond our own worlds: A first step in envisioning equitable practice. In C. Genishi & A. L. Goodwin (Eds.), *Diversities in early childhood education: Rethinking and doing* (pp. 253–269). New York: Routledge.

Louis, R. (2005). Performing English, performing bodies: A case for critical performative language pedagogy. *Text & Performance Quarterly, 25*(4), 334–353.

Macedo, D., & Bartolomé, L. (1999). *Dancing with bigotry: Beyond the politics of tolerance*. New York: St. Martin's Press.

Mandala Center for Change. (2009). *The Mandala Center*. Retrieved May 7, 2009, from http://www.mandalaforchange.com/welcome.htm

McLaren, P. (2000). Paulo Freire's pedagogy of possibility. In S. Steiner, H. Krank, P. McLaren, & R. Bahruth (Eds.), *Freirean pedagogy, praxis and possibilities: Projects for the new millennium* (pp. 1–22). New York; London: Falmer Press.

Medina, C. (2007, February). *Performative literacies: Towards a critical analysis of embodied practices.* Keynote address presented at the National Council of Teachers of English Assembly for Research, Nashville, TN.

Mitchell, T. (2001). Notes from the inside: Forum theater in maximum security. *Theater, 31*(3), 55–61.

Mohanty, C. T. (1989/1990). On race and voice: Challenges for liberal education in the 1990s. *Cultural Critique, 14*, 179–208.

Moll, L., & Gonzalez, N. (2004). Beginning where children are. In O. Santa Ana (Ed.), *Tongue-tied: The lives of multilingual children in public education* (pp. 152–156). Lanham, MD: Rowman & Littlefield.

Moreno, J. L. (1978). *Who shall survive?: Foundations of sociometry, group psychotherapy, and sociodrama* (3rd ed.). Beacon, NY: Beacon House.

Nieto, S. (1999). *The light in their eyes: Creating multicultural learning communities.* New York: Teachers College Press.

Nieto, S. (2007). Foreword. In G. Campano (Ed.), *Immigrant students and literacy: Reading, writing, and remembering* (pp. xi–xii). New York: Teachers College Press.

Obidah, J. E. (2000). Mediating the boundaries of race, class and professional authority as a critical multiculturalist. *Teachers College Record, 102*(6), 1035–1060.

Ochoa, G. (2007). *Learning from Latino teachers.* San Francisco: Jossey-Bass.

Ochs, E., & Capps, L. (2001). *Living narrative: Creating lives in everyday storytelling.* Cambridge, MA: Harvard University Press.

Ochs, E., Smith, R., & Taylor, C. (1996). Detective stories at dinnertime: Problem solving through conarration. In C. Briggs (Ed.), *Disorderly discourse: Narrative, conflict, and inequality* (pp. 95–113). New York: Oxford University Press.

Parsons, T. (1959). The school class as a social system: Some of its functions in American society. *Harvard Educational Review, 29*(4), 297–318.

Pineau, E. L. (2002). Critical performative pedagogy: Fleshing out the politics. In N. Stucky, C. Wimmer, & I. NetLibrary (Eds.), *Teaching performance studies* (pp. 41–54). Carbondale, IL: Southern Illinois University Press.

Porfilio, B., & Yu, T. (2006). "Student as consumer": A critical narrative of the commercialization of teacher education. *Journal of Critical Education Policy Studies, 4*(1). Retrieved February 22, 2007, from http://www.jceps.com/index.php?pageID=article&articleID=56

Rhedding-Jones, J. (2002). English elsewhere: Globalization, assessment and ethics. *Journal of Curriculum Studies, 34*(4), 383–404.

Rohd, M. (1998). *Theatre for community, conflict & dialogue: The hope is vital training manual.* Portsmouth, NH: Heinemann.

Rust, F. (1999). Learning lessons about diversity: The role of field experiences in the preparation of teachers. *Journal of Early Childhood Teacher Education, 20*, 175–179.

Rymes, B. (1996). Rights to advise: Advice as an emergent phenomenon in student-teacher talk. *Linguistics and Education, 8*, 406–437.

Rymes, B. (2009). *Classroom discourse analysis: A tool for critical reflection.* Cresskill, NJ: Hampton Press.

Rymes, B., Cahnmann-Taylor, M., & Souto-Manning, M. (2008). Bilingual teachers' performances of power and conflict. *Teaching Education, 19*(2), 105–119.

Saldaña, J. (2005). *Ethnodrama: An anthology of reality theatre.* Walnut Creek, CA: Altamira.

Saldaña, J. (1995). *Drama of color: Improvisation with multiethnic folklore.* Portmouth, NH: Heinemann.

Sanders, M. (2004). Urban odyssey: Theatre of the oppressed and talented minority youth. *Journal for the Education of the Gifted, 28*(2), 218–241.

Sarsona, M. W., Goo, S., Kawakami, A., & Au, K. (2008). Keiki steps: Equity issues in a parent-participation preschool program for native Hawaiian children. In C. Genishi & A. L. Goodwin (Eds.), *Diversities in early childhood: Rethinking and doing* (pp. 151–165). New York: Routledge.

Schutzman, M., & Cohen-Cruz, J. (Eds.). (1994). *Playing Boal: Theatre, therapy, activism.* London: Routledge.

Schutzman, M., & Cohen-Cruz, J. (1990). Selected bibliography on Augusto Boal. *The Drama Review: A Journal of Performance Studies, 34*(3), 84–87.

Schweitzer, P. (1994). Many happy retirements: An interactive theatre project with older people. In M. Schutzman & J. Cohen-Cruz (Eds.), *Playing Boal: Theatre, therapy, activism* (pp. 64–80). London: Routledge.

Shor, I. (1987). *Freire for the classroom: A sourcebook for liberatory teaching.* Portsmouth, NH: Heinemann.

Shulman, J., & Mesa-Bains, A. (1993). *Diversity in the classroom: A casebook for teachers and teacher educators.* Hillsdale, NJ: Research for Better Schools and Lawrence Erlbaum Associates.

Sizer, T. (1973). *Places for learning, places for joy: Speculations on American school reform.* Cambridge, MA: Harvard University Press.

Sleeter, C., & Bernal, D. D. (2003). Critical pedagogy, critical race theory, and antiracist education: Implications for multicultural education. In J. Banks & C. M. Banks (Eds.), *Handbook of research on multicultural education* (2nd ed.). San Francisco: Jossey-Bass.

Souto-Manning, M. (2005). *Critical narrative analysis of Brazilian women's schooling discourses: Negotiating agency and identity through participation in culture circles.* Unpublished doctoral dissertation. University of Georgia, Athens, GA.

Souto-Manning, M. (2007). Education for democracy: The text and context of Freirean culture circles in Brazil. In D. Stevick & B. Levinson (Eds.), *Reimagining civic education: How diverse nations and cultures form democratic citizens* (pp. 121–146). Lanham, MD: Rowman-Littlefield.

Souto-Manning, M. (2009a). Acting out and talking back: Negotiating discourses in American early educational settings. *Early Child Development and Care, 179*(8), 1083–1094.

Souto-Manning, M. (2009b). Negotiating culturally responsive pedagogy through multicultural children's literature: Towards critical democratic literacy practices in a first grade classroom. *Journal of Early Childhood Literacy, 9*(1), 53–77.

Souto-Manning, M. (2010). *Freire, teaching, and learning: Culture circles across contexts.* New York: Peter Lang.

Souto-Manning, M., Cahnmann-Taylor, M., Dice, J., & Wooten, J. (2008). The power and possibilities of performative critical early childhood teacher education. *Journal of Early Childhood Teacher Education, 29*(4), 309–325.

Spolin, V. (1999). *Improvisation for the theatre: A handbook of teaching and directing techniques* (3rd ed.). Evanston, IL: Northwestern University Press.

Spry, L. (1994). Structures of power: Toward a theatre of liberation. In M. Schutzman & J. Cohen-Cruz (Eds.), *Playing Boal: Theatre, therapy, activism* (pp. 171–184). London: Routledge.

Sternberg, P., & Garcia, A. (2000). *Sociodrama: Who's in your shoes?* (2nd ed.). Westport, CT: Praeger Publishers/ Greenwood Publishing Group.

Subalusky, W. (2006). *The observant eye: Using it to understand and improve performance.* Charleston, SC: BookSurge Publishing.

Szeman, L. (2005). Lessons for theatre of the oppressed from a Romanian orphanage. *New Theatre Quarterly, 21*(4), 340–357.

Taussig, H., & Schechner, R. (1994). Boal in Brazil, France, the USA. In M. Schutzman & J. Cohen-Cruz (Eds.), *Playing Boal: Theater, therapy, activism* (pp. 17–32). London: Routledge.

Telesco, G., & Solomon, A. (2001). Theatre of the recruits: Boal techniques in the New York police academy. *Theater, 31*(3), 55–61.

Tollefson, J. W. (1991). *Planning language, planning inequality: Language policy in the community.* London: Longman.

Tom, A. (1997). *Redesigning teacher education.* Albany, NY: State University of New York Press.

Valenzuela, A. (1999). *Subtractive schooling: US-Mexican youth and the politics of caring.* Albany, NY: State University of New York.

Warren, J. T. (1999). The body politic: Performance, pedagogy, and the power of enfleshment. *Text and Performance Quarterly, 19,* 257–266.

Weinblatt, M. (2006, March). *Introduction to the Theatre of the Oppressed & multicultural-multilingual dialogue.* Workshop conducted at meeting of Teachers for English Language Learners, Athens, GA.

Weinstein, C. S., Tomlinson-Clarke, S., & Curran, M. (2004). Toward a conception of culturally responsive classroom management. *Journal of Teacher Education, 55*(1), 25–38.

Wolfson, N. (1998). *Perspectives: Sociolinguistics and TESOL.* Boston: Heinle & Heinle Publishers.

Wooten, J., & Cahnmann-Taylor, M. (2007, November). *Acting out: Performance techniques for new teachers and their students.* Paper presented at the annual meeting of American Council on the Teaching of Foreign Languages (ACTFL), San Antonio, Texas.

Zentella, A. C. (2005). *Building on strength: Language and literacy in Latino families and communities.* New York: Teachers College Press.

Index

About the Authors

MELISA "MISHA" CAHNMANN-TAYLOR, PhD, Associate Professor of Language and Literacy Education at the University of Georgia, is interested in the relationship among language, culture, literacy, and power. She studies bilingual education and multilingual classrooms as sites of social conflict, where possibilities exist for social change, justice, and democracy. She recently coauthored (with Richard Siegesmund) *Arts-Based Research in Education: Foundations for Practice*, which argues for hybrid forms of qualitative inquiry that embrace traditional methods alongside nontraditional, feminist, poetic, narrative and arts-based approaches. She has published her poetry, scholarship, and scholARTistry in journals such as *Anthropology & Humanism, Teachers College Record, Educational Researcher, Language Arts, Linguistics and Education, Anthropology and Education Quarterly, Women's Review of Books, Journal of Latinos and Education, Critical Inquiry in Language Studies*, and *American Poetry Review*. She won the 2004, 2005, and 2008 Dorothy Sargent Rosenberg prize for poetry and judges the annual poetry contest for the Society for Humanistic Anthropology.

MARIANA SOUTO-MANNING, PhD, is Associate Professor of Education at Teachers College, Columbia University. From a critical perspective, she examines the sociocultural and historical foundations of early schooling, language development, and literacy practices. She studies how children, families, and teachers from diverse backgrounds shape and are shaped by discursive practices, employing a methodology that combines discourse analysis with ethnographic investigation. Her work can be found in journals such as *Early Child Development and Care, Early Childhood Education Journal, Journal of Early Childhood Research, Journal of Early Childhood Literacy, Journal of Research in Childhood Education*, and *Teachers College Record*. She was awarded the American Educational Research Association (AERA) Language and Social Processes Early Career Award in 2008, the AERA Early Education and Child Development Early Research Career Award in 2009, and the National Conference on Research in Language and Literacy (NCRLL) Early Career Award in 2009.